# Endorsements

I write (primarily) fiction, so I'm accustomed to action-packed stories. Nothing, however, could have prepared me for Sherrie's true-life thriller, *Faith on Fire*. Loaded with unexpected plot twists, conflict and redemption, this amazing book kept me riveted from the first page to the last. Sherrie's captivating writing style will hook you, too. Whether you're dealing with difficult relationships, bias in the workplace or personal/spiritual struggles, there's something in these pages for you. Highly recommended!

—**Janice Thompson**
Author of over one hundred novels and non-fiction books,

Sherrie's book, *Faith on Fire*, is a must read for anyone considering a career in the fire service, both male and female. Her story of the challenges she faced and overcame as the first female fire fighter in the Dallas Fire Department is at times shocking and at times humorous. But throughout it is her story of determination, perseverance and faith in the face of great obstacles to succeed in her chosen life's work. I am proud to have had Sherrie work with me and to be my friend.

—**David Baker**
Deputy Chief, Dallas Fire Department (Retired)

Sherrie Wilson is a trail blazer and a true leader. As the first female hired on the Dallas Fire Department she endured excessive agitation and the vengeance of some defiant men firefighters to embark on a career in the fire and emergency medical services (EMS). Through her experiences and inspirational messages she has carved a path that others can follow professionally or personally. Thanks for letting me ride your coat tail because I get to experience the impossible and witness the miracles.

—**Trixie G. Lohrke**
Battalion Chief, Dallas Fire Department

Change is many times not requested, often times it is dreaded or neglected, but it is inevitable. My chosen profession was the fire service, a profession steeped in tradition, pride, trust in each other, and fellowship. For well over one hundred years, firefighters were all male. The job is demanding and challenging in many ways physical, emotional, psychologically. The men that chose this line of work are well aware of this and most are prepared to rise to any challenge. Not to sound silly, but you could almost smell the testosterone at the fire station. Then in 1977 a major change in our city's Fire Department came along . . . a woman! Sherrie was assigned to the same station and shift that I worked at that time. I hired on the department in 1968 and had ten years of experience under my belt when she broke the gender barrier. I worked for another thirty years until retiring in 2008. With this tenure I got to see and be a part of what was probably the biggest change that this department had experienced since its inception on July 4, 1872. This book was written from the heart of an individual who took a gigantic leap of faith against all odds to achieve a goal that most thought was impossible, many thought was crazy, and some who to this day still think that women have no place in the fire service. Read her story about the good, the bad and the ugly that comes with trying to prove to yourself and to 1,400 men that you have got what it takes.

—**Pat Murphy**
Captain (retired), Dallas Fire Department

Back in the 1970s if you had a heart attack in Dallas, you, by chance, would have the best EMS /paramedic respond to the scene. As you are laying on the ground and hear sirens coming and the paramedic running you would most likely see Sherrie Wilson, EMT-paramedic from the Dallas Fire Department. Sherrie was the first female in the Dallas Fire/ Rescue. Sherrie worked for years in the department, proving herself many times over as "the first." In thirty-five years of leadership and service in the Dallas Fire Department, she engaged her talent as incident command technician, PIO, training officer, driver-engineer, recruiting officer and as well as having fulfilled numerous other responsibilities. Sherrie's business, Emergency Management Resources, prepares employees to handle a broad scope of challenges in the health and safety arena. Sherrie is guest editor for *Industrial Fire World* magazine's EMS column. She has saved many lives herself through teaching skills to save a life. It's been a privilege to be her mentor and friend watching her develop her full potential.

—**David White**
President, Fire and Safety Specialists& Publisher,
*Industrial Fire World* magazine

Sherrie captures the spirit and is a model for women working their passion in a male-dominated environment. Lessons learned from these experiences will serve women and men today and far into the future . . . lessons of faith, giving your best, respecting those you serve, and bearing the brunt of whatever comes mixed with faith that God is with you is success by His definition. I admire the self-directed but not self-serving commitment to become a tremendous example for women in any career.

—**Lynn Bourland White**
CFO and Marketing Director, *Industrial Fire World* magazine

One would expect a wild ride of a tale through the eyes of one of Texas' first feminists. Instead we are humbled by the story of a person who never gave up on a dream. From a young girl faced with a situation most parents fear explaining, to a young woman filled with determination and faith, Sherrie finds herself thrown into a world where feminine strength means nothing. Sherrie faces fires that are unworldly only to return to a world in which she was just the same as everyone else. Will she break and pull the girl card to reach the top? Or will she tough it out and play a man's game? Suspenseful, frustrating and yet inspiring, *Faith on Fire* captures the essence of humanity and the power of faith . . . on fire.

—**Heather Bliss**
BS Behavioral Neuroscience, graduate student,
the University of Mississippi

# FAITH
## ON
# FIRE

Published by Redemption Press, PO Box 427, Enumclaw, WA 98022. Toll Free (844) 2REDEEM (273-3336)

Redemption Press is honored to present this title in partnership with the author. The views expressed or implied in this work are those of the author. Redemption Press provides our imprint seal representing design excellence, creative content and high quality production.

ISBN 13: 978-0-9968791-0-1 (Print)
        978-0-9968791-1-8 (ePub)
        978-0-9968791-2-5 (Mobi)

Library of Congress Catalog Card Number: 2015936707

# DEDICATION

To the awesome men and women of the Dallas Fire Rescue Department: You create miracles out of impossible situations for the citizens of Dallas, Texas.

Sam, I know there is a God, and I believe he loves me because he sent you to be by my side through life. You are my true gift from God. You are a man of integrity, gentleness, kindness and love. You have been my strength, my stabilizer, my source of contentment. As a woman in a man's world, I relied on you as my sounding board, my sanity and my discernment. You spoke into my life positively and breathed life into my goals and desires. You lifted me when I was broken, and we have shared in all that life has to give. This book is dedicated to you, my love.

To my children Johnathan and Grant: How precious you both are to me. You have been a source of overwhelming joy. You were our reason for working hard and long hours. We wanted the best for your life. The overwhelming success you both are today gives me contentment and peace. My precious grandchildren bring such pleasure to our lives. We love you and will always reserve a place in our hearts for our gifts from God.

To Anya, my precious Russian daughter (Dorcha): God loved me enough to give me a daughter later in life. He could not have picked a better one. You have stood by me in business and became a key partner, a trusted friend and my family. I am so blessed you are in my life. Thanks for all the shredding.

To Joseph my oldest brother, Gerrie my womb mate, Susan my little sister and Lillard my little brother: You have all been my best friends through life. Thank you for standing by me and putting up with all my fast-paced, hair-on-fire, get-r-done way of being. You know all the good, the bad and the ugly, yet you continue to love and support me. Thanks for all the edits.

To my precious mother and daddy: Thank you for your example of faith, determination and love. I serve an awesome God because of your influence in my life. I am an author because of my mother, and my success is due to mimicking her hard work. Thank you to God for giving me both of you as parents. You have been my blessing. Daddy, my memories of your joy and laughter are things I cling to.

To Sherry Wendling, my best friend in life: You are one of life's best teachers and coaches. Thank you for being a real friend in the face of all life deals you. I learned, "The more you do, the more you can do," from watching you. Most importantly, you taught me how to be a giver because you gave so much to me. We have shared family and friends, ups and downs, celebrations and failures and yet, our friendship thrives. You are a gift from God.

# CONTENTS

# ACKNOWLEDGEMENTS

From the beginning of my career, I wrote in a journal. Being so inspired by the opportunity to live out my dream as a rescuer, I had to capture the impossible and the miracles. I wish I had captured more than I actually did, however, I only used 70,000 words out of over 400,000. While capturing my life, I was not a great writer at the time. Not even a good one. Thank God, I had people in my life who contributed to the success of this book.

Eileen Key was one of the first editors I met along the path to writing. Eileen took my journals and made them come alive with stories. Eileen is a professional writer, editor and proofreader and she has written more than thirteen books and is mother of three and grandmother of five. www.eileenkey.net

Athena Dean Holtz is the publisher at Redemption Press. Not only is she a publisher, she is a friend. I have witnessed some awesome miracles in her life which inspired me to craft my book around impossible situations and miracles. I have been inspired by her integrity. Athena and her staff, including editor Neva Cole, provided some of the final edits to my book and provided excellent feedback. www.redemption-press.com

Heather Bliss is meticulous editor. She asked questions and forced me to go into my book and explain things that non-firefighters would not understand. She did all this while encouraging me with the wisdom of someone much older than herself. I cannot thank Heather enough for her warm-hearted consideration and support. She is now my number one editor! www.emresources.net

# PREFACE-THE RIDE OF MY LIFE

All I could do was climb and hold on for dear life. A hint of blood, smoke or flame—let the code 3 ride begin.

From the beginning, I climbed steep, daunting hills toward saving lives, only to face a plummeting drop into the presence of death, frustration and defeat. There were double loops through the blistering heat of agitation and sudden stops that threw me directly into the middle of gender and racial curves. Tossed side-to-side, this wild ride provided unique opportunities to love and admire those whom I could've easily resented.

Some relationships jerked me up and then catapulted me face down. Teasing drove me to a point where my brain felt as if it was being slammed back and forth against the insides of my skull. At times, I could not think—and could barely hold onto my faith. I was left bloodied, broken, both physically and emotionally, and the force of constant stress challenged my body's ability to recover.

It was amazing to witness extraordinarily vigorous stands for brotherly love and feel the unique and powerful grip of friendship. I became a sister inside a big family of brothers, uncles, dads and grandpas who shared their joy for living life as rescuers and a winning attitude could not stand in the face of our attack, but the last room was raging like a loose wild animal. Through the walls it sounded like a bloody animal battle, and it was my turn to fight. I swallowed hard, inhaled sharply and kicked in the door. Standing just inside the gates of hell, one-on-one with fear, I met the roaring breath of the devil himself. I could hear my heart beating inside my chest. I prayed for strength.

*This one has some personality.*

My enemy snorted and charged. I bowed up, gritted my teeth and charged with all the boldness of a saint in Zion, waving my nozzle down the devil's throat. The shrieks and sizzles quickly turned to steam.

Science proves every droplet of water hitting fire expands 1700 times its volume creating steam. A scorching wet heat—a watery blanket capable of boiling my lungs—would have consumed me had it not been for my mask. The room became strangely quiet.

*Is the beast retreating or lying quietly for the right moment to attack? Was it regrouping, or getting ready to blow?*

Although my partner was near, I felt alone. You always feel alone in the midst of smoke, heat and far-reaching darkness. The heat tests resolve and determination. Darkness tests faith, and I was going to have more than my fair share of testing today. I called on God for help—I always have.

Firefighters taught me that winning takes faith and belief even when uncertain of the outcome. They were right. I have never seen a fire that would not go out. You either have faith or you don't. Believing in miracles is the ultimate test of one's faith. Fire fighting comes in as a close second.

Orange-red fingers of fire reached out through the room and pointed at me in a teasing manner. The fire retreated again and then came hissing and slithering like a multi-dimensional snake, its fangs ready to sink into my flesh. Each wave of fire increased with intensity until explosive. Finally, the fire flashed, roared, and then rolled above my head. I hunkered down, turned my nozzle to full fog fountain (holding a nozzle straight up, and the spray comes down around you like an umbrella shield of water), summoned my faith and prayed.

My pastor, George Hancock at Christian World Church in Richardson, Texas, once told me "The first ingredient of a miracle is an impossible situation." Through my years of facing the impossible, I have certainly seen many miracles in my career, but are these words true?

*Is the impossible required for a miracle?*

These stories reveal the answer.

## Stoking My Faith

It has been said there are specific events in life that have such a powerful impact on you that they shape your life and character. At the ripe age of eight, this was one of those events, which would in some strange and complex way influence my future, my life choices, and my destiny.

There were five of us kids, along with mother and dad, packed in an old blue Rambler station wagon with fake wooden panels. A family of seven and, according to my mother, seven was also God's favorite number.

We were headed to Grandma's house at the beginning of another hot, sizzling, Texas summer. The sun reflected through the car windows; there was no air conditioner, creating a stifling sauna-like heat. With the windows rolled down there was not enough air movement to provide relief from the torrid temperature. The traffic on the old two-lane farm road stood at a standstill.

My sweaty, long brown hair stuck to the sides of my face and neck in globs. Beads of sweat rolled down my forehead and into my eyes. Restless, I moved my lips up against the car's rear window and blew my hot steamy breath creating a small circle of fog. With my finger, I carved out a smiley face and then leaned back and grinned with satisfaction at my childish work of art. Of course, that was life at the age of eight—childish things.

Life was carefree. My only concerns were playing with my brothers and sisters and visiting my grandparents. My summer would be spent on the farmland with my two sets of grandparents in central Texas. I tasted a lot of central Texas dirt when picking tomatoes in the morning while it was cool. My afternoons were spent cooling down with my brothers and sisters in a galvanized #2 washtub filled with water. That was the way life was meant to be at my age—then everything changed. All the stifled traffic was caused by an accident up ahead.

A lifeless body slumped over the steering wheel of a badly damaged car—the driver's door swung wide open. As our old station wagon approached, the man inside the mangled car became fully visible. His chocolate brown hair looked wet and matted—a bloody mound. The right side of his head rested against the steering wheel, his face toward me. I inhaled sharply. A large and bloodied gash ran across his forehead. I watched blood trickle down one side of his nose, across his lips and drip down his chin. In dazed curiosity, my eyes locked on him. Suddenly he gasped like a dying fish opening its mouth for the last time.

Alarms went off in my head. I wanted to swallow but could not produce any saliva. I felt the muffled and distant sound of my heart racing away in my chest. It seemed to beat faster as I watched his mouth, waiting for him to breathe again—but there was nothing.

A single drop of blood began bubbling up on the edge of his chin. I inhaled another big gasp of air, all the while willing him to breathe. The bubble grew and doubled then popped into thin air. The leftover blood formed a tear growing bigger and bigger, until finally separating. The white sleeve of his shirt framed the slow-motioned blood all the way out of my sight.

A mustache of sweat rolled on my upper lip; I wiped it with the back of my hand and swallowed hard.

*Breathe.*

My heart continued to pound inside my chest. No one told me the bloodied man was dead, but somehow I knew. I had just witnessed death. The image of death for an eight-year-old could have been devastating but not for me. I had no fear while looking at the man or his slowly coagulating blood. I was curious because of the dead-fish last breath.

Our car inched forward in the traffic, and I lost sight of the bloodied man and woke up from my slow-motioned gaze. I realized many cars had stopped along the side of the road. I twisted around only to see blurred outlines of adult-sized bodies pointing at one another. None had any clear definable face, but it appeared their mouths moved in a slow drama-like fashion. I watched in curious shock as not a single person moved, but they were pointing and blaming one another.

*It is your responsibility! No, it is yours!*

I was upset, most by the adults frozen in fear.

*They did nothing!*

They stood with their feet planted firmly on the ground. They might as well have been in graves themselves, because they were no use to anyone. It was as if they were unable to move. Why would they not help?

*Was he really dead?*

I thought the man might be dead, although I'm not sure I realized what *dead* was at the time. I once had a blue parakeet that died, and I buried him in the backyard. I cried while saying a prayer that Pepe go to parakeet heaven, but this accident was very different. I understood this to be real danger and peril. It was something I had never experienced before. This was life and death hanging in a delicate balance.

Suddenly my life was no longer about spending the summer at my grandparents' house or fighting with my brothers and sisters as to who would go first in the #2 washtub. My life was transforming into something very serious and treacherous. I lacked my previous feeling of safety and security. A multitude of emotions washed over me. The strongest was anger.

As our car chugged up a hill, I cried, "Daddy we have to stop and help the man!" My father just kept driving. I protested again. I begged, "Dad, stop the car! We have to help that man!"

My father glanced back and said, "Nope, we'll just get in the way."

With tears running down my cheeks, I cried out, "Dad! No one is helping that man! We should stop and help him!"

My father just inched along with traffic. I grew frustrated and felt helpless at his lack of concern. I wanted to take some action, but I did not know what to do.

*Someone should try and do something!*

I sat back in my seat with my arms crossed, turned my lower lip down and pouted while holding back tears of frustration.

My mother sensed my disappointment. She turned to me, reached for my hand, and looked me in the eye. "The Bible says where any two agree in prayer and ask in Jesus name, it will be done."

I grabbed her hand, bowed my head, and with all the gusto an eight-year-old could muster, I asked, "Jesus, help the bloodied man."

It was one of those short, sweet and to-the-point kind of prayers. Mine always are.

Mother had agreed with me, and I swallowed hard and began to feel a little better.

I looked back at the accident scene, I fully expected to see people in action, but my view was blocked. I whined about not knowing what was happening.

Mother said, "Have *faith*."

"What's faith," I asked.

"Well, it is when you trust that whatever the answer is, it is the best answer. God takes care of His children," mother said while stroking my hair.

I thought about what she said, and I am not sure I understood, but I was determined to have this *faith* thing. It was all I could do.

I reclined in my seat with questions.

*Have faith? Okay, I will do it if it helps this man.*

Then I heard something. I cocked my head to listen harder as if listening harder was possible. My ears perked up, and I heard it in the distance.

*A siren!*

Mother smiled and said, "See, God answered your prayer already. He sent an ambulance. It is your miracle!"

I stood up and pointed at the ambulance which was now topping the hill, then danced a jig right there in the back seat. It was a self-expression only a child could create. It was a celebration of life and death wrapped into one big ball of excitement.

*Faith! Yes faith. I like it!*

As the ambulance grew closer, the siren got louder, and my pulse began to race again. It was as if all the sadness, blood, people, thoughts, prayers and faith were stuffed into a bag and then exploded into thin air. I relaxed, leaned back in my seat and mouthed "Thank you, God."

*Miracle!*

Only seconds later, Mother said, "Look, look." She pointed at the flashing lights within a few feet of us.

I was suddenly more alert and reenergized. I gazed out the window with delight. I began to jump up and down with wild enthusiasm, excited that someone was willing to help the man.

*Yahooooooooo! It is a miracle!*

The ambulance slowed down due to the heavy traffic. As it got even with our car, I studied the old Cadillac hearse that doubled as an ambulance. The curtains were open, and you could see a stretcher in the back. "Lawrence Funeral Home" was stenciled on the side window in big gold letters outlined in black. Two people rode in the front seat.

As the ambulance became even with our Rambler, I saw the driver's face.

*Papaw!*

It was the man who lovingly and happily bounced me on his knee and called me his, "little-copa-teeling-lindaling-sugalin-dumplin." It was my grandfather, Papaw Bozeman, and he was a man of joy!

Papaw worked part time for the funeral home in a small, rural community. I remember beaming and feeling proud of him. I danced and jumped in celebration because now someone I knew and loved was part of this first miracle in my life.

My father told me to settle down. I replaced all the movement with a big smile, teary eyes and a lump of pure admiration in my throat.

The only thing that mattered now was the man was going to be helped. Somebody was willing to help. I had found my first hero in life—my papaw!

It is one thing when a child is told to have faith, but it is a quantum leap to see a horrible accident, pray a prayer and have that prayer answered immediately. I not only gained a hero, I realized that God hears our prayers.

*I think God likes me!*

This event on that sizzling summer day may seem insignificant, but it began a domino effect in my life. On that day a seed was planted inside me, and it began to grow. This drama, this problem, would be transformed into my future of facing the impossible and witnessing many miracles throughout my life.

What mattered to me on this day was what was missing at the accident—action, pure unadulterated action. Being action-oriented is woven into the very fabric of my being.

To witness death—watching, waiting, caring and helping during life, death, gasping last breaths, tears of sorrow and separation—would certainly be in my future. This experience from my childhood, this death, the end of this man, was a beginning for me. It began as an awakening about life and death, heaven and hell, good and bad. My life changed that very instant, and I was no longer the child, I had been before. I was transformed into a curious, watchful and more aware child. I asked endless questions and wanted to know far more than necessary about life, illness, and death.

I still think back to that event when it is hot outside and my hair sticks to my skin. Reliving the event is tamed in my mind now, because I am warmed by the satisfaction of knowing what to do when people need me. There will be no eight-year-old little girls crying, sticking their lips out and pouting on my watch.

From front to back: Sherrie, Lillard, Susan, Santa, Gerrie, and Joseph

## Kitchen Fire

It was summertime and my mom and dad were at work, which left us five kids home alone. Being the oldest daughter, I got to play mom to the other children. I woke to the smell of bacon. I rubbed my eyes and walked lazily into the kitchen. Lillard, my four-year-old little brother, was standing in a chair in front of the stove with a spatula in his hand. He smiled wildly. His big blue eyes sparkled.

For the longest time my little brother could not pronounce my name. He said proudly, "Sherdie, I am cooking breakfast!"

Susan, my little sister, stood beside him and chimed in, "Yeah. We are cooking you breakfast!"

They were proud of themselves for doing something helpful. I smiled back still in a sleepy fog. I groggily turned to watch the television.

Suddenly, I smelled something burning. Before I could stand up, I heard high-pitched screams and the pitter-patter of little feet running toward me. I turned to see the frying pan flash-fire up toward the Vent-A-Hood.

In a blink, the yellow-orange flames grew and crackled upward. Black smoke began to bellow and bank down from the ceiling. My brother and sister looked to me for direction and protection.

"Jesus! Oh my God! Susan, go wake Joseph and Gerrie! Get them out of the house," I screamed.

Lillard clung tightly to my leg, so I peeled him away and shooed him outside. I turned and raced out the side door to our neighbor's house. I ran so fast, my feet barely touched the tightly woven grass. I banged on the neighbor's door and yelled for help.

She opened the door and I huffed, "Kitchen is on fire! The kitchen is on fire!"

The neighbor followed me back to the house and we entered the side door. Smoke was banking down from the ceiling about a foot.

Our neighbor approached the sink, grabbed a lid, and placed it on the burning pan. The fire was immediately snuffed out.

*Miracle!*

For a minute we both bent over and put our hands on our knees to catch our breath and slow our throbbing hearts. Everything then became a blur.

The fire department showed up—Engine 46. My older brother, Joseph, had called Mom and she rushed home from work.

Mom talked to a tall, white-haired firefighter who smiled and winked at me saying, "Quick action prevented the house from burning down." He pointed to the blackened cabinet and ceiling. "We checked the attic, and the fire stopped here. You should be okay now," he said.

He placed his helmet back on his head, nodded goodbye, turned and then left. All the other firefighters followed him out.

As the firefighters left, a sick feeling came over me. I had faced a fire—an impossible situation. Since the day of the car accident, I wanted to relive that powerful moment of faith; however, miracles seemed to come at the expense of impossible situations.

## Life's Oxidizing Agents

The Dallas Independent School District rolled out integration of public schools over a period of years. I heard the expression *bussing* on television as a young child, then I saw a man with a big Afro hairdo, wearing tight jeans and platform heels. He was marching with a sign while demanding, "Fairness and equality." He seemed really angry.

So I asked Mother, "Why is that man so mad?"

Mother said, "Black people are not treated as equals with white people. He is fighting for equality and wants to bus children to different schools."

*Bus?*

"You mean like in a school bus," I questioned.

"Yes! Just like a school bus. They want to desegregate kids—mix up the schools so that things would be equal among everybody."

Shaking my head, confused, I did not understand. Mother was using some mighty big words.

The protestor was Al Lipscomb. He became an activist and political figure who was battling for opportunities for minorities inside the city of

Dallas, Texas. Our paths were destined to cross in life as Al, a future Dallas city councilman, would one day become my boss. In the meantime, Al introduced me to the idea that things in life were not always fair. Al was an oxidizing agent. Oxidizers are not themselves combustible, but they support combustion when combined with fuel. I would be an oxidizer too. I would come to understand Al and his struggles with a twist—a uniquely feminine twist, but they were struggles just the same, and we both would fan the flames in different ways.

Although I did not know at the time, Al and I had something in common. We stood for what we believed in: the rights of others, especially the underdogs or those mistreated. Al would stand for black people, push for bussing, and scream and yell for equality among races. I remember watching Al closely as a child. I had never really seen anybody that upset except when I got into trouble.

Watching Al, I learned that people noticed the squeaky wheel. The media loved him. People listened to Al, and eventually they would do what he wanted. Because of Al and his push for bussing, my life was now stirred with a racial and gender flavor that gave depth to my thoughts as a child. I began to wonder what it would be like to go to school and have friends of color.

As a child I had limited experience with others of a different race, but I knew they were children of God. Grandmother told me, "We all belong to God." She sang a song about red, yellow, black, and white, they are precious in his sight. Finally in middle school, I experienced the bussing phenomenon, which allowed kids from other areas of town to be bussed to my local school, therefore integrating black and white children.

Racial and gender flavor would be inflamed again later in my life. It did not take long for the first stirring. There was a boy bussed to my middle school who cornered my twin sister in the stairwell and tried to kiss her. I suppose that is what any boy would do at that age, but because of this incident, we moved from Dallas to Duncanville, Texas. My parents also wanted to escape the effects of a volatile atmosphere caused by those opposed to integration. By default, I became the product of white flight.

## Duncanville High School

Duncanville High School was the home of the Panthers. The girls' basketball team was called the Pantherettes, and we were known for bringing home state championships. This is where I learned some of the most important lessons I needed to enter the fire service.

Coach Sandra Meadows was a short and stocky female with short, gray-white hair and a deep, raspy voice. Her kind eyes let you know immediately she cared about you as a player and a person. She had a heart for God: we prayed before and after every practice and game.

However, playing for Coach Meadows was not easy. She was tough and bellowed at us much like the male coaches did the boys. Being part of the Duncanville Pantherettes was the hardest and most challenging thing I had ever done in my life. At the end of practice, completely exhausted, we ran the basketball lines till our legs burned. I wobbled off the court every single morning. We worked out so hard my legs sometimes ached throughout the school day.

*Why do we have to push so hard?*

It was as if Coach Meadows knew what I was thinking and would say, "Pushing through the pain is what separates the winners from the losers."

*Can't we take it just a little easier?*

Coach would bellow out, "Pantherettes are not wimps. We are champions and we play and practice like champions!" When I thought I could not go any further, coach would remind us, "There are those that think they can and there are those that think they can't. They are both right!"

Coach Meadows also told us to have faith. "We are champions, and we will win," she said with determination.

*We did!*

The adults in my life were seeing to it that I lived out every ounce of my potential energy. Come nightfall, I secretly dreamed about leaps of faith and miracles.

"So we fix our eyes not on what is seen, but on what is unseen, since what is seen is temporary, but what is unseen is eternal."
—2 Corinthians 4:18, NIV

Dedication: This story is dedicated to all the coaches and mentors in the world that lift up while squeezing youth to become the best that they can be.

## Ignition Point

The summer after graduation from high school a friend had left his position with an ambulance company to return to college. We had taken the first aid class together, and I was looking for a job. I decided to use the opportunity of him returning to school to ask for his job.

Little did I know the ambulance service I worked for in the summer of 1977 had a contract with the Dallas County medical examiner. We were paid twenty-five dollars for each dead person we transported to the morgue. I was disheartened when I discovered my job of saving lives really meant picking up the dead on the streets of Dallas. Papaw and I had something else in common. We both saved lives and carried the dead. It was a difficult and disgusting job. We transported some of the most mind-numbing carnage that included gunshots, stabbings, overdoses, and suicides. We hauled them all: day after day of stiff, bloodied, blue, and smelly bodies. I felt dirty and nasty at the end of each shift. The job itself was an impossible situation and a miracle rolled into one big ball of work.

God was beginning to show me a glimpse of my future. The pieces were all beginning to fit together, and the importance of saving lives was becoming a desire. On a few rare occasions, I did get to save a few lives, but even that was a little rough in the beginning.

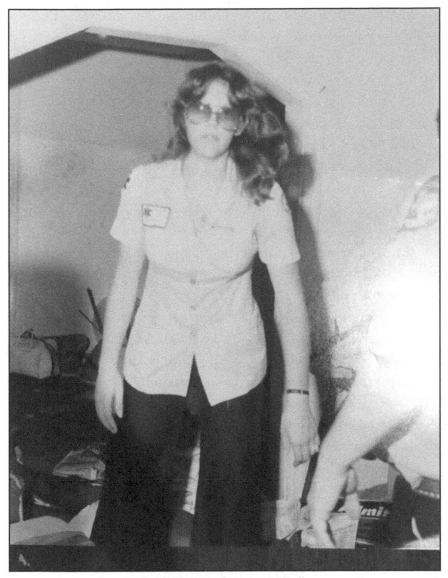

Sherrie at a murder scene in Dallas

My first ambulance partner was a man named Bullet. Bullet was a likeable guy. He was pot-bellied, balding and had one wild eye that jumped when he was excited. Bullet was a little on the nervous side. Bullet took me under his wing and taught me everything he knew about riding the ambulance. I appreciated his generous spirit.

My first run was in an old Cadillac ambulance, just like my grandfather drove when I was eight years old. I felt I had arrived when I first climbed into that Cadillac. I held my head high and beamed with nearly the same satisfaction I had after my papaw helped the bloodied man. I hadn't even saved anybody yet! But it was only a matter of time before that day would come.

Bullet and I were called to transport a lady from a nursing home to the hospital. She had a urinary tract infection and was having some trouble breathing. Her catheter bag held cloudy and dark brownish-colored urine. The lady moaned with every move we made toward the stretcher.

I tried to encourage her. "Hang in there," I crooned softly. She just moaned all the more, so I shut up because I really did not know anything else to do.

In route to the hospital, Bullet made a wrong turn. He pulled into the driveway of a house then backed out and headed the way we had just come. We made the block and pulled into another driveway. He reversed again and headed back the way we came.

*Hmm . . . What's going on?*

On a scale of one-to-ten, Bullet's panic level climbed from a three to a nine. He turned and looked at me, his wild eye darting back and forth.

"I'm lost!"

We were headed to a hospital in Grand Prairie but got lost on a residential street somewhere in Irving.

In the middle of Bullet's panic attack, I noticed the lady started sucking air like a dying fish. I sat up like I was going to do something for her and hollered, "Bullet, she's not breathing!"

Bullet's wild eye started jumping more, and he looked apprehensive and alarmed. Anything I said to him received the response: "Well, well, well, hang on. I will help you when we get there."

*Impossible situation!*

I realized I should not have said anything to Bullet because it only escalated his nervous behavior. He seemed to have developed a tick in addition to the already jumping eye. Also, I was not too sure about what to do for the lady but pray.

*God, help Bullet settle down before he strokes out. And while you're at it, help me with this old lady too.*

Suddenly, I recalled something from my first aid training class. I reached down, and I lifted the old lady's chin, opening her airway. She snorted and took a breath. I watched her chest rise and fall.

*Thanks, God.*

When I reported her breathing to Bullet again, he sighed in relief and then pulled over and stopped. He turned off the lights and siren. The sun had gone down, and we sat quietly in a faint light from the blue horizon. Bullet inhaled deeply and paused.

*What's he doing now?*

Bullet flipped a switch. The windshield wipers came on. He turned the wipers off and tried another switch. The radio came on. He turned the radio off, sighed, and mumbled something under his breath.

*I think Bullet prays too.*

It was easy to understand why Bullet flipped all those switches because there sure were an awful lot of them built into the ceiling of that old Cadillac. Bullet finally flipped on the inside lights and jerked a map out of the glove box. He studied it a moment, scratched his head and then said, "Ohh-kay," followed by a big sigh.

Bullet spun the map upside down and studied it some more, and then he spun it back to where it originally had been. He looked to the north and then to the south trying to figure out where he went wrong. He rubbed his chin in deep thought. He put on a pair of cheater glasses, held the map closer to his face and squinted at the fine print. He looked up and studied the street sign. A glance in the rearview mirror showed me his wild eye was still jumping. He looked back at the map in a serious manner.

Bullet finally seemed to get his bearings. He reached up and flipped the switches back on and the ambulance began to wail and whine and lights began to flash. We headed west onto Airport Freeway toward our destination.

*Finally! I am saving lives. Well, sort of.*

While I watched Bullet study the map, I had dropped the lady's airway. I soon realized that the lady's breathing was contingent on me holding her airway open. I lifted my elbow up on the stretcher, arched my back and tried to get comfortable. There was certainly no room to save anybody in the back of that Caddy.

After more than an hour of "the scenic route," we finally made it to our destination. The patient was still alive, and we checked her into the hospital and washed up. I remember standing in the bathroom and thanking God for helping me with my first patient. I met Bullet outside the bathroom, and we walked quietly toward the old Cadillac.

In the middle of the parking lot, Bullet paused and put his hand on my shoulder like a father would a son. His face serious, his wild eye was now under control.

"I only took one wrong turn, and it really was not a big deal," Bullet said seriously.

I just smiled and nodded.

Back in 1977, a first aid card was all one needed to ride an ambulance. *Thank God, that has changed.*

Thinking over my first run, it was obvious that I had a lot to learn. I vowed then and there that I was going to learn more than just first aid. I needed to learn the streets, where all the hospitals were, and I needed a lot more education. I needed a leap of faith.

*There are those that think they can and there are those that think they can't. They are both right.*

That run was a turning point for me in several ways. A desire was getting stronger, and I was beginning to see what I wanted to do with my life.

*God, I need to go to school, and I do not have any money. Thanks in advance.*

Late one night, all the ambulances were parked in the bunkhouse at the same time, and my co-workers and I sat around talking. This was a rare occasion because we were usually busy transporting back and forth around Dallas County from the nursing homes—well, when we weren't picking up dead people. During this conversation we all lounged around telling jokes and laughing at one another. I watched them all quietly. People shared snacks and poked fun at one another and then someone asked, "What do you want to be?"

I perked up.

Others around the room started to share their life goals, and then the question was directed to me. I did not even think about it, I blurted out, "I want to be a paramedic. I want to save lives! The morgue runs and nursing homes are so boring and . . ."

"You cannot do that!" One of my male co-workers was now pointing directly at me. "You have to be a fireman first, and women *cannot* be firemen!"

The room roared with laughter. I was in the middle of sharing one of my most deeply-seated and important goals, in addition, he was rude and interrupted me!

*Impossible!*

I did not know being a firefighter had become my passion too, at least not until challenged.

With nothing more to say, I just sat furious, reeling, and frustrated. I had been laughed at—he was purposefully being obnoxious, and no one in the room stepped up to defend me. In all fairness, they did not really know me either. To add insult to injury, they all believed women could not be firefighters. I could tell it in their eyes. They looked at him as though they agreed with his every word.

It was difficult enough to hear what he said, but it was even worse that I could not think of a response. I was mad at him for trying to steal my dream. I was mad at myself for not having the nerve to say anything back. I fumed all night long. I tossed and turned in my bed thinking and planning.

*"The mind is not a vessel to be filled, but a fire to be ignited."– Plutarch*

Our ambulance had answered a call with the Dallas Fire Department earlier that day, and I got to know a few of the paramedics and firefighters. They were nice compared to this *guy* at the ambulance company. They seemed friendly, like they somehow believed in me. I was attracted to the way they lived their lives—as rescuers.

At 0700, I was relieved of duty. I was now on a mission, and you would not have wanted to get between my goal and me.

*I'll show him!*

I went home, took a shower, looked for a copy of my college transcript, made a quick phone call for directions and headed to the Dallas Fire Department headquarters located at 2014 Main Street in the heart of downtown Dallas.

## Free-Burning Destiny

Standing in front of the door at the recruiting office, I paused, inhaled deeply, released a breath mixed with a prayer, and threw my shoulders back. With my head up I marched confidently into the office. Coach always told me since I was the tallest member of the team, I needed to stand tall so the opposing team would worry. Today, I did it so that I would look like a good team member. A small slender female in uniform looked up toward the ceiling and greeted me with a strong handshake.

*Okay, a female in uniform. This is a good sign.*

The recruiter was a fire inspector. I told her I wanted to be a firefighter and a paramedic and I was here for the job. I said it like it was no big deal because I just assumed I would be perfect. Standing six feet tall, I had broad shoulders, a slim waist and a long set of arms and legs. My athletic build was coated with a can-do spirit.

Pat looked up at my Amazon-sized body. She shook her head as if she did not believe what she was seeing and hearing. She directed me to a chair in her office.

She explained the Federal Justice Department was pressuring the fire department for not having any female firefighters.

Her eyes judged me, but her voice said, "We really need to get a female hired."

Confidently I said, "I am the one!"

She smiled and hesitated, "No female has successfully passed the tests before. Sixty women have taken the test, and all of them failed."

*Impossible! I bet a Pantherette can do it!*

She painted a bleak picture of my odds of getting hired.

We sat quietly for a moment, and then she asked, "What angle do you have working for you?"

My mind raced to find an angle. I thought about my grandpa the load-and-go mortician of yesteryear. I thought about the house fire and running to my neighbor for help. I thought about the firefighter patting my head and winking at me after the fire. I could not tell her I am here to show up a guy who basically challenged me on whether I could become a paramedic and firefighter.

Then I heard myself say, "I am a Duncanville Pantherette! I served under Coach Sandra Meadows. I can do anything!"

She probably thought, "What the heck is a Duncanville Pantherette, and who the heck is Coach Meadows?" But she released a big wide smile, and we started filling out applications and scheduling tests.

Not long after completing the civil service exam, I was scheduled to take the physical agility test. This was the big one—the one no female had passed.

The physical agility exam required me to pick up a wall ladder and take it around the side of an A-framed structure and place it upon the roof. Then I had to climb to the highest pitch of the roof, pull the ladder up, and maneuver it around and down the opposite side of the roof.

*Piece of cake for a Duncanville Pantherette!*

I carried a 150-pound dummy up several flights of stairs and back down.

*No problem; I lifted weights in high school and college.*

Advancing a charged hose line several hundred feet was no problem.

*Easiest thing I have done so far. What Duncanville Pantherette could not do this?*

Finally, I coupled sections of larger hose lines together and dragged them several hundred feet in one direction. I ran back to the other end and dragged it back to where I started.

*When does the difficult part start? Coach Meadows was harder on me than this.*

I sat winded and waited for the next test.

A cocky officer came and reached for the mask on my back. I loosened the old leather belt straps, slid the mask off and handed it to him. He asked for the rest of the turnout gear, so I removed the coat, boots, and helmet and handed them over. I had finished the physical agility test with time to spare.

When facing the impossible, certainty is a distinction all its own. Certainty of mind, mixed with faith, belief, and expectation makes for a powerful miracle in life. Somewhere, somehow I had made the decision this job was mine! There was not even a doubt. There was not even a maybe. It was a free-burning certainty of *faith*—it was my destiny. Nothing would stop me. Not a test, not a man, not anything!

*Miracle!*

Feeling excited, I moved on to the lie detector test. I never have had much faith in these devices, especially since it said I was lying about having played basketball. Women's basketball is serious business in Texas! The arson investigator testing me explained that my love of basketball caused a strong reaction to the question.

He continued the test and asked, "Have you ever worn women's clothing?"

"Yes, I wear them all the time," I said with a wink and flashing a smile.

He shook his head and mumbled something about, "Changing the test questions."

"Have you ever had a relationship with another man?" he asked.

"Yes! Plus, I have two brothers and a father. I like them too," I said smartly.

They were not prepared for me. It was not long until that test ended.

In October, 1977, wearing a yellow suit with a silk blouse, I was ready to face the interview panel. I threw my shoulders back and walked self-assuredly into a conference room filled with chief officers. There were five old, wrinkled, serious-looking uniformed men sitting at a conference table. One man waved me toward a seat. Questions were fired off about my life, my family and my beliefs.

Every time I answered a question, they turned and looked at each other. Some smiled, some shrugged, and I caught one bald-headed guy rolling his eyes. I was not sure if they were looking at each other because my answers were right or wrong. I had no idea what they were thinking, but the department needed to hire women to meet the Justice Department requirements. In 1972 the Equal Rights Amendment was passed by congress and declared there would be no inequality on the grounds of gender. I was a product of this era, and I had a desire to serve. I was oblivious to how much they needed me. It was clear I needed the Dallas Fire Department to reach my goal of being a rescuer, but they needed me too. The questioning continued.

They had asked me about how wives would take the news of a female in the fire station. Being naïve, I thought they would like me. I was ignorant of many things, including the presence of my own athletic, fit, and strong body. I was absolutely clueless how other women would see me. I began to understand through this questioning that some wives would see me as a threat.

Like every other female in the world, I wanted to fall in love and get married too. I never thought about it until one of the chiefs asked me what would I do if I fell in love with a firefighter.

"If he is the one, you cannot stop true love," I said honestly.

*More eye-rolling.*

Being young and inexperienced, I could really only say I wanted the job. I started out wanting to be a paramedic, but since you had to be a firefighter too, I thought *why not?* A good job seems like a good thing for a girl like me.

Finally, one member of the brotHERhood needed to quietly confer with the other member of the brotHERhood in order to ascertain whether they all approved of me. One particularly gruff man with a well-endowed crooked nose shooed me out of the room so they could talk about me behind closed doors.

*Thank you, God. I think I got this job. I am stretching my faith.*

Respecting the tradition of going through the process was in the back of my mind, but we all entered this meeting knowing what would need to happen.

My certainty of purpose in life felt electrifying.

After what seemed like an eternity, someone finally opened the door and waved me back inside. When I entered the room some of the men were smiling. I do not remember anyone saying anything, but somewhere along the line, I understood that I was now a uniformed member of the Dallas Fire Department. Among all the questions and funny looks, they decided something positive about me. The impossible situation was I needed a good job, and the Dallas Fire Department needed a woman for the job. The miracle was that I was ready for my new destiny.

*Thank You, God! You're awesome!*

When each man reached out his hand to welcome me aboard, I passed on the handshake and gave them each a hug. My actions quickly welcomed them into a world of women in the fire service. I wondered if my hug made them want to reconsider their decision. Maybe my hugs raised a few eyebrows, but in the background somewhere was a little glimpse of hope and happiness for me and a new future for the Dallas Fire Department.

*Miracle!*

Another miracle was that the department paid all my expenses for training at the fire academy and for medical school to become a paramedic.

*Double Miracle!*

In addition, they paid this little Duncanville Pantherette like they would a man.

*Wasn't even expecting this—triple miracle!*

The icing on the cake: I even had a pension.

*Wasn't expecting this either—quadruple miracle!*

When asking God for a way to get training for this job—*he* delivered a quadruple miracle better than I could have dreamed.

> *"Now to him who is able to do far more abundantly than all that we ask or think, according to the power at work within us."*
>
> —Ephesians 3:20, ESV

To this day, I do not know if I was considered for the position because they thought I was a good candidate, or because the Justice Department was breathing down their necks.

*Who cares! I am proud to have this job and I am thanking God for it!*

Sherrie with Chief Dodd Miller at press conference

## Fire Academy

The Dallas Fire Department has a rank structure. It starts at the lowest rank, cadet, and then on to rookie, private, second driver, driver-engineer, lieutenant, captain, battalion chief, deputy chief, assistant chief, and at the very top is the chief of the department. Cadets are considered bottom feeders where some firefighters are concerned. We were the lowest of the low. Cadets work part time while going to school and finishing up college requirements. I was a cadet—and a female.

*Is there anything lower than a cadet and female?*

I reported for duty at Communications inside Old Central Fire Station, a rickety station converted into administration offices. As a cadet, my half-day on duty was spent as a glorified car washer for the chief's cars and errand girl for the top dogs. Maybe they wanted to keep a close eye on me.

The department held a press conference to introduce me to the media. Everyone seemed overly excited that they finally had a female pass all the tests to become a firefighter.

*What's the big deal? I need a job, and people get excited?*

Within a month and a paycheck, I bought myself a new car. I was thrilled and told some of my new friends in the fire department about it. One guy told me he wanted to see my new car. So when we got off duty, we walked toward the parking lot. When he saw my little blue Monza, he frowned. I looked at him thrilled and excited but suddenly questioned his sour face. He squinted in the sun, brought his hand up to shade his eyes and then locked eyes with mine.

"Girl, you should not have bought this car!"

"Why not?" I asked.

"Because, there is not a chance in hell you are going to make it through the fire academy!"

He talked like he knew something that I did not know, like there was some big secret out there about me. He stomped off with nothing else to say.

*Impossible! My life is filled with people who want to steal your dreams!*

My certainty was not deterred. I got inside my new car and peeled out of the parking lot.

My faith felt threatened, but my determination was fully engulfed with flame. With purposefulness, I reported to rookie school.

Rookie Class 181 started on June 19, 1977, and I was excited. Well, I was excited right up until I arrived. It was like a new recruit getting off the bus at Army basic training and Captain Jack, one of the academy instructors, greeted us with a bark.

He yelled, "At a fire is not the time to learn discipline! Discipline starts now! You will not argue! You will not debate! You will only obey!"

*Oh geez! What have I got myself into?*

Captain Jack was a ruggedly handsome man but frowned and yelled so much that you did not get to see the good-looking side of him. Instead, I was afraid of him. This was my first real taste of the paramilitary side of my new life. Captain Jack reminded me of Sergeant Carter on *The Gomer Pyle Show*, except he was not funny—he was serious. He meant business! He stood and moved with his hands placed firmly on his hips. His feet were spread for balance with an arch in his back. He bent forward slightly and looked up at you as he let out expletive after expletive. We froze, afraid to move. At first I wanted to cry, but with clenched teeth and tight jaw muscles, I prayed the berating would soon end.

*I am about to pee my pants!*

Captain Jack would say two decibels louder than normal, "If you can take it, you can make it!" I also recalled Coach Meadows doing her fair share of screaming some of the same things at our basketball team. The only difference was I knew she was *for* me. With Captain Jack, I did not know if he supported me or not.

Captain Jack was originally assigned to my class, but they swapped him for Captain Tray at the last minute. It was rumored that management did not trust Captain Jack to see me through to success because he was so rough and tough talking. Over the years, I have gotten to know Captain Jack, and I hold him in high regard. He was tough on all of us, and I am clear that his job was to acclimatize us to the paramilitary world. He held me to the same standards as everyone else, which helped me maintain credibility and ultimately caused me to thrive in the academy. The same treatment of all the rookies worked in my favor. I was seen as not only capable to do the job, but I also did not expect any favors—this created respect among the brotHERhood of rookie firefighters. Eventually, Captain Jack seemed to acknowledge the fact that I did not just want the title, I could actually do the job. I kept up. But after all, I had already been trained by the best of the best as a Duncanville Pantherette.

Three things got me to this level of success, my parents, my faith in God, and my coach, Sandra Meadows. Feeling the burning in my legs was not new to me. Being yelled at was not new to me. Working hard and pushing past the pain was not new to me. Standing strong in the face of difficultly was becoming the norm for me. All these things, along with those two instructors at the academy, helped to build my character and confidence. To them I am forever grateful.

*The more you do, the more you can do.*

Captain Tray, now assigned to class 181, was at the opposite end of the spectrum from Captain Jack. Captain Tray carried himself differently. He talked softly, but firmly. He cared not only about our ability to fight fire and save lives, he also cared about our souls.

*He is just like Coach Meadows!*

Captain Tray said a prayer before every meal, and he told us that he ran his fire station that way too. We were required to be respectful to God around Captain Tray. Cursing was not allowed. This was firefighter tradition he told us several times.

*Mom and Dad can relax; the fire department has normal people.*

After morning workouts, we had to shower and prepare for class. There were no separate facilities for women, so the guys all went first showering, and I always went last. While the guys were taking their turn in the bathroom, a pair of lacy lavender underwear was stolen from my locker. I know this because I found them flying just below the American flag when I went out to lower it one day.

*Impossible!*

One young firefighter greeted me all excited and asked if I was mad and was I going to tell on them. I looked at the panties and back at the rookie inquisitively. He was bold when he told me about my panties flying with the flag but now looked sheepishly at me, hoping I would not tell the training officers. I did not want to cause a problem for my co-workers, so I negotiated respectful behavior in the future. Once I had a promise that no one would break-and-enter my locker again, I had mercy and agreed not to tell. Plus, I was thankful they used clean panties.

*Double impossible and miracle rolled into one!*

Then there was burn night. Burn night is when we move from the classroom to the burn building. The plan was for the officer to set fires for us, and we would go in and put them out. My partner and I knelt down waiting for the signal to enter the burn building. We went "on air," nodded in agreement and entered. My partner went in first, then me, followed by my captain who pushed us closer and closer to the fire. Suddenly, my partner stood, screamed and ran out, leaving me to fight the fire alone. I took over the hose line and put the fire out with my captain behind me. After the fire was out, I approached to see if my partner was okay. I thought maybe he had been burned. He had broken a cardinal rule: He left me alone, and this did not line up with our buddy system.

With his head down and no eye contact he said, "I'm sorry."

*Impossible! That was it? No excuse? Nothing to say?*

Somehow I knew he would not make it in the fire service, and he flunked out of emergency medical technician (EMT) school. I soared through rookie school, EMT and paramedic school. Fire fighting was an impossible situation for him, but it was an exciting ride and the ultimate miracle for me.

Dedication: This story is dedicated to all the academy instructors throughout my career. They not only trained me in the beginning. In-service training is a valuable part of keeping a firefighter safe and knowledgeable.

# Chapter 2

---

# ROLLOVER

Definition: Rollover is unburned combustible gases released early, accumulate at the ceiling, and are pushed under pressure into uninvolved areas. When these gases mix with oxygen, they ignite, the gases burn and the fire rolls over the ceiling.

## Fire Station 3

Heads turned, eyes froze, but no one said a word. I had arrived at Dallas Fire Station 3 and introduced myself. "Hi! I'm Sherrie Clark," I said in my sweetest cheerleader voice.

October 20, 1978, was a landmark day for the fire department, as I was the first female firefighter to be placed in service. Glances and nods were thrown my way. I had practiced and rehearsed the job many times, but I had never practiced walking in and introducing myself. I stood there alone, my twenty-year-old mind wondering what would happen next. I was lost in a sea of nameless faces.

Suddenly, a firefighter burst through the vented doors of the game room, smiling, and eager to check me out—he was my captain. His eyes studied my face then traveled up and down my six-foot frame. He walked around to check out my backside like a rancher inspecting a cow. I felt a little self-conscious, but stood with my head up and shoulders back, posturing proudly. I knew inspection was part of my first day, but I did not know it would be so close of an inspection.

This was his firehouse, filled with his men, and now he would take charge of me. He'd been selected as the captain over the first female firefighter.

Capt. flashed a smile. "You're a vixen."

"What's a vixen?" I asked. The room chuckled.

"A female fox," Capt. replied smiling.

I smiled, thinking that was sweet.

Another firefighter spoke up saying, "Capt., she's cuter than a freckled face pup under a red wheel wagon." The nameless firefighter smiled with his eyes twinkling, but he was talking to and looking directly at Capt. Capt. nodded his head in agreement.

Blushing, I wasn't sure what to do with the attention.

Capt. smiled, stepped closer to me, into my intimate zone, and sniffed my hair and neck. I thought for a moment I was going to get a welcome kiss. I could smell his aftershave. He smelled clean.

His sparkling eyes looked directly into mine as if searching for something. Suddenly I felt nervous and bit my lower lip, casting my eyes down and away from his intense gaze. Not sure what to do, I just stood there, speechless, then looked back up and into Capt.'s eyes.

Capt. moved in even closer, bent his knees forward and positioned his knees, one on each side of my right leg. He began to hump, quiver, and ride my leg while wearing a devilish grin. Like a deer caught in headlights, I stood frozen while his eyes danced and sparkled. He continued to hump.

His curly red hair brushed against my face as he finished humping me and stepped back with a satisfied grin. Everyone in the room waited for my reaction.

I gestured toward his legs. "Are you finished?"

He let out a nervous laugh while saying, "Yes, just seeing what kind of sport you are!"

"Oh, I'm a good sport, there's no question there."

Capt. winked at me and said, "Well then, welcome to Fire Station 3."

All the men in the room released sheepish smiles and relaxed. I shrugged my shoulders, rolled my eyes and stepped back away from this powerful man who totally and completely held my attention. With my heart pounding in confusion, I laughed back, relieved that the interaction was not mean or hateful.

Capt. waved me off to my lieutenant, as he was finished with me for the moment. The lieutenant introduced me to everyone. Some men were friendly and offered their hand and others just nodded in my direction and seemed to keep their distance.

My impossible was now possible, and the miracles can begin.

Like a thoroughbred dancing nervously at the gate, I anxiously awaited for the house bells to hit. There would be no delays. No hesitations. No uncertainty. I was finally ready to be placed into service for the citizens of Dallas. It was truly a miracle. All the years of wanting, needing and desiring the opportunity to serve now came together for me in one tumultuous moment. Being the one to place the lid on the fiery skillet or rip people from the jaws of death, was now dependent on one last thing—the sound of the alarm.

Having learned what I needed, I now deserved my chance at this job, this life, this opportunity. I wanted it. I had wanted it since childhood.

*Ralph Waldo Emerson once wrote: "Do not go where the path may lead, go instead where there is no path and leave a trail."*

Having had no idea that there was no path, I put one foot in front of the other and starting walking through this career. There was no trail to follow or a path to lead me, and I tripped and fell at times, but I just kept walking.

My tour of the station included my assigned bathroom which was located in the apparatus room. It had only a toilet and sink and no heat in the winter or air in the summer. It gets hot as Hades in Texas during the summer, and hordes of mosquitoes are always seeking water sources. This bathroom was that water source. I did not really like using this restroom because being confined with mosquitos was a challenge, but in order to keep the peace, I said nothing and bought insect spray.

My second shift on duty, I discovered my bathroom had been decorated with pink drapes, a pink rug, and magazines with pictures of naked men. Had the upper echelon known of my welcome, I am sure heads would have rolled, but I found the attention humorous and rolled my eyes, thinking I was blessed to have such an awesome job! Due to some of the playfulness, there seemed to be a little sexual tension at times, especially with so many handsome men around, but it required us all to keep our focus on the job, forgive some of the antics, and this I was more than willing to do. Forgiveness was easy when I was young and impressionable, but it would become more difficult in the future—the very near future.

Every shift, the men left their lockers open and proudly displayed pictures of naked women. I soon learned not to leave my locker unlocked. Somebody left me a gift—my own calendar with pictures of naked men. Evidently, they did not want me to feel left out. I blushed, rolled my eyes and just considered it an anatomy lesson.

*Impossible!*

A few shifts into my new job, I approached Capt. in his office. He looked up and said, "What do you want Clark?"

"I just want to talk to you a minute Capt."

"Shoot!"

"Well, on day one you humped my leg. I understand it was funny and all, but Billy and Joe think that it's OK to hump my leg because you did it. I really want this job, and I want to be thought of as a professional. I don't feel like a respected part of the team when my teammates are humping . . ." Capt. cut me off.

"You're right! I shouldn't have done that. I will take care of this."

"Yes sir."

That night at the dinner table, Capt. stood and announced, "Guys, on day one I humped Sherrie's leg, and it was pretty funny. She is now a member of our team, and we are going to show mutual respect to our team members. So we ain't going to be humping her leg anymore."

"Yes sir," the members said in unison.

I said, "Ok," and shrugged my shoulders. The leg humping ceased for the most part.

## First Fire

Pat was the driver-engineer on the Mobile Intensive Care Unit 703 (ambulance), but we called it "The Box." I was assigned to Engine 3, but as a paramedic, I would take turns with the Bubbas riding the box. Pat had enthusiasm and joy like my dad and papaw. He could easily establish espirit de corps, and the other firefighters respected him. He had a gentle, good humor and optimism about women in the department. His wonderful outlook made my life much easier in the beginning. I made my first fire and my first ambulance run with Pat, and they could not have picked anyone better to train me. His happy heart was infectious. We both mounted on Engine 3 early in the shift, and the bell hit—we got a fire. Pat winked at me in assurance. I looked back at him with fear in my eyes after seeing thick black smoke rising in the distance. Pat yelled over the loud engine, "We are gonna beat this fire down! It is already out, girl! You hear?" Pat declared victory even before we faced the fire. All the men at Station 3 had this positive, winning attitude about every impossible situation we faced as a team.

*I love it here!*

We showed up at an apartment fire where fire was coming from the first floor, but smoke was puffing out the eaves of the roofline above the second floor. Pat and I entered with a hose line. We crawled around in the dark smoke and sprayed water on a small fire. We sat still waiting for the fire to show itself again, but nothing happened. We crawled forward hoping to find more fire and smother it. From the corner of my eye, I saw red. I nudged Pat and pointed and we focused on what we both thought was fire. I opened the nozzle and soon realized water was now spraying out a window taking the smoke with it. Immediately I heard screaming. Pat told me to shut off the water, and I did as instructed. This is when we realized we were spraying at the red lights flashing on top of a police car that sat out in front of the building. An officer had obviously gotten wet too, because he was cursing up a storm and complaining about his wet uniform. Pat and I lay on our sides laughing until our captain came to the door and hollered for us to come outside. We had created a ruckus. We stepped outside sheepishly, and Capt.'s eyes sparkled as he put his finger to his mouth and pointed us away from the angry officer.

*Geez! Will they fire a rookie for this?*

Capt. took me upstairs and showed me how the truck crew was cutting the fire off in the attic while we were putting out the fire below. His intention in this lesson was two-fold: teach me something about firefighting and save me from the police officer who was requesting someone's hide.

Sherrie at her first fire

After the officer dried off and cooled down, Pat and I showed up nonchalantly at the engine and removed our bunker coats. It was the first time anyone had seen a woman firefighter at a fire scene in Dallas, Texas. When removing my bunker coat and pants, I revealed my hot, sweaty, tall, slender, and muscular body. There was a brisk coolness to the air. I had an athletic build and the confidence of youth, and it showed. All eyes were on me, and I heard some firefighters inhale deeply while others exhaled longer than necessary. One of the police officers groaned under his breath. I suddenly felt self-conscious.

Unknowingly, I had created another ruckus. I was greener than a gourd's gut about firefighting, but I did sense the unnecessary attention, and quickly headed to put my coat back on. Remaining smooth on the surface, my mind was peddling like hell underneath as how to redirect the uncomfortable attention.

*Impossible situation!*

Thinking fast on my feet, I pointed at Pat and said aloud, "He's the guy that wet you down." Suddenly, all eyes and attention were directed at Pat. Quickly I holed up in the apartment with Capt. for another lesson on firefighting. Pat faced the gun-toting officer alone, feverishly defending himself.

*Hilarious miracle!*

Pat turned out to be one of my top agitators, and I was his, but together we had fun, and I appreciated his joy for life and his faith and contagious winning attitude.

It was not long after we arrived back at the station, and the bell hit again. In route, Pat assured me, "We got this!" He had a magnificent obsession with winning; it was habit forming. I was beginning to understand this awesome winning attitude of firefighters—*faith on fire.*

Fire showed in the window of an upstairs apartment. I stretched the hose line, and we quickly knocked the fire down. The fire started in a closet, which is a typical sign of arson. Inside the closet was a mound of clothing smoldering—a motionless hump of blankets. We began pulling the clothes and blankets out of the closet and soon found a mother and her two children: a boy and girl.

*Impossible!*

The arsonist and murderer was a boyfriend who had beaten them unconscious. To cover his crime, he threw them in the closet and covered them with clothes and blankets. Methodically, he poured gasoline on the pile, struck the match and *poof,* their lives ended; they were no longer necessary.

When we found the dead bodies, my captain shooed me out of the room and commenced to worry; he acted as though he had to be overly protective of me. He did not want me to see those burnt bodies. The Bubbas followed orders and tried to keep me out of the room too. Finally, I cornered Capt., and I told him about my job riding the ambulance and carrying the dead for the medical examiner all summer.

"I have seen burnt bodies before," I assured him.

I told him about responding to a fire in west Dallas where the entire family died of smoke inhalation and when the fire reached the baby laying in a crib, the heat drew the baby's arms upward as if needing to be picked up by his mother. It struck me as painful at first, and then I found myself just going through the motions as if I had seen hundreds of bodies like this before.

*I guess I am not your average girlie-girl.*

Today was a dark day and a brightly lit day all rolled into one twenty-four hour, exhausting shift. I learned that the winning attitude sees problems as opportunities that challenge ability and determination.

*It was a miracle day for me!*

Capt. promptly quit worrying about me being able to take the horror side of this job of saving lives, and I was allowed to operate full-throttle alongside some awesome friends and brothers.

Walking up to Station 3 today you will see to the right of the entrance door a piece of wood that has axes, helmets and other firefighter type symbols on it. It has been painted to welcome you to Station 3, but there is a story behind that piece of wood because it replaced what was at one time, glass. Basically, my leg got humped one too many times at Station 3, and I gave a slight shove to the firefighter doing the humping. Well, it was more than a shove and he fell backwards through the glass, off the porch, across the sidewalk and onto the grass in the front yard. I was not really mad, just a little frustrated and worn out. The good news is that we fixed that broken glass, and it has welcomed people to Station 3 for nearly thirty-five years. No one got in trouble, no letters were written and all the players that contributed to that incident are now safely retired.

Entering paramedic school was a thrill for me. Several of my rookie school buddies and I would meet up and ride together studying and testing each other. One rookie school friend was black, one Hispanic, a white guy and myself. We were all smart and serious about our schooling. A neighbor of mine questioned me on why I rode to work with men. I looked at her inquisitively wondering what she was talking about.

She pressed me, "Won't your parents be ashamed if they know your spending time with men, especially black and Hispanic men?"

*Impossible!*

Shaking my head in defiance I said, "These are my friends! They got my back, and I got theirs. That is something you don't understand and never will! My parents would be upset with me if they thought I didn't treat my co-workers as human beings.

This person excused me from her life and decided I wasn't friend material.

*Bussing was seen as an impossible situation, but maybe it did have a positive impact on the children that experienced it. I am proud to live and work with my friends, co-workers and fellow citizens.*

## Delivering a Fly

My paramedic internship was spent at Station 11 located in the heart of Dallas, at Cedar Springs and Lemmon, just north of downtown. The area is an eclectic mix of gays, yuppies, and some of the super-rich of Dallas. Along the west side of this area, near Harry Hines, are lower income apartments. I served them all, happily.

The call came in as an "emergency childbirth." We slid the pole, raced to the box, and sped toward the scene. Entering the seedy apartment building near Harry Hines, I hauled it up the stairs, leaving my preceptors (trainers) behind in my excitement to deliver my first baby. The door to apartment number twelve was unlocked.

It was about zero dark thirty, and all the lights inside the apartment were out. I checked all the wall switches and nothing worked. I guessed they had not paid the bill, because lights were on in all the other apartments. I pulled out my penlight and moved around the darkened apartment. I checked the bedrooms, bathrooms, hallway, and kitchen. I was not expecting to find anyone in the dining room but a moan stopped me in my tracks.

A very pregnant Hispanic female was on a small cot up against the wall. She was in labor and was ready to push. Her labor pains came in waves of less than a minute. Her belly tightened like a clamp squeezing the baby out. My heart skipped a beat, and I was thrilled to be a part of helping bring life into this world.

All I had was a penlight with me. To make the penlight work, you had to pinch it between your fingers. I needed both hands to deliver the baby, so I put the penlight in my mouth and squeezed down with my lips. I disrobed the female so that I could deliver the baby. My preceptor finally caught up with me and handed me the OB kit.

The baby was beginning its final descent down the birth canal—crowning. I was ready in my quarterback stance, waiting for the little bundle to arrive.

As this baby started to deliver, I noticed what was coming out was tubular shaped. I thought for a moment that I was dreaming.

*Impossible! Hmmm . . . something is not right here.*

I had not delivered a baby by myself, but I had witnessed enough that I knew what should be happening. And this was not it.

*Geez! Maybe I am not ready to delivery my first baby, because this is not a baby!*

It looked like a larva as it delivered. I looked at my paramedic preceptor trainer sheepishly and then back at the non-baby baby coming out.

*Impossible!*

Suddenly, a pair of feet dropped down. It was a breech birth and the larva appearance was really the butt delivering first.

Once the mother delivered the baby, I swaddled it up and looked into its tiny eyes. It was definitely a baby.

My preceptors loaded up the patient, and I snuggled that baby close. It was my first baby to welcome to the world.

*Joyous miracle!*

## The Box

"Sherrie! It is your turn to ride the box!"

We rotated riding the fire engine, fire truck, and box. Taking your turn on the box meant mounting up with your fire gear and all. The fire gear was used for backing up the Bubbas at fires or heavy rescues requiring extrication at major accident scenes. Riding the box was an incredibly unique experience, because you got to enter in every type of home and work place. You really got to see how other people lived out their lives.

However, when riding the box, you began to feel like a machine. One run after another, in a rapid-fire sequence, adrenaline racing through your body, then the bone-crushing weariness sets in. Sometimes we stayed up all night and others we would go to sleep and wake up many times over. Riding the box always made it a challenging drive home. I got pulled over by a police officer one morning. I am sure he thought I was probably drunk because of my weaving. I was just exhausted. My duty uniform and bloodshot eyes served as his clue.

A technique used during war times to break a prisoner's spirit and get them to talk is to let them fall asleep and then wake them over and over.

I was broken at times for sure. The most disturbing thing about the job of paramedic is this same agitating sleep-interruption-sleep pattern. My mind was at war because of an ounce of sleep sandwiched between runs.

*Impossible!*

This lack of sleep caused severe burnout in our medics. Burnout affects attitude, and attitude affects performance. Proper performance is imperative for quality service during emergencies. Getting sleep away from the station became my miracle. At times you could get a second wind, but most of the time, paramedics are working on an uncompromising lack of sleep. The problem is that when you are firing at warp speed, it is hard to slow down and relax.

The bells rang at Station 3. I stood and slapped a piece of sausage in between my biscuit and wrapped it in a napkin. In a dead run, I gulped and choked down what was left of my breakfast. Swallowing the last bite, I opened the door to the box and climbed in.

Turning right out of Fire Station 3, we headed east onto Gaston. We slammed on our brakes, squealing our tires while attempting to stop for a blue Honda pulling out in front of us at Haskell Avenue. I flipped a knob, and the siren went from a wail to a yelp, intended to alert the driver, but he drove on ignoring us and clueless to our presence. I looked at my partner and we both rolled our eyes and thanked God we did not broadside the baby blue Honda.

*Who drives a baby blue Honda?*

We took off again, crossed Fitzhugh Ave, and took a left into an apartment complex.

In the parking lot, three pint-sized children speaking Chinese in high-pitched screams met us. One little girl appeared to be the group leader. She grabbed my hand and pulled me up a flight of stairs while yelling what was gibberish to me.

We stepped inside a room filled with floor to ceiling sheets dividing the room into separate areas. Behind each sheet were more sheets. The floor was also covered with sheets and blankets; they were makeshift beds.

Each sheeted area was home for a different family. Sometimes as many as eight families pitched in together and split the cost of an apartment. Electricity was not a problem—none used air-conditioning. It was always hot and miserable inside those apartments.

The little girl pulled back the first sheet and pointed for me to enter. Her words were unintelligible, but I knew a patient must be in here somewhere. I stepped inside. The place smelled odd, like incense, but also stale.

Behind the second wall of sheets, a pregnant female was unconscious and curled into a ball. She was having a seizure and the maze of sheets and blankets below her were damp—her water had broken.

Dropping to one knee, I checked her pulse; it was bounding. She inhaled deeply and stopped seizing. I rolled her onto her back and opened her airway. She was still breathing. A quick check of her blood pressure revealed 190/110. Exactly what I feared: she was suffering from pre-eclampsia. Pre-eclampsia is a pregnancy-related condition that includes elevated blood pressure and protein in the urine. This is when the blood pressure becomes very high and accompanied by an altered mental status, pre-eclampsia becomes dangerous to the mother and child. About the only option is delivery of the baby.

My partner headed back to the ambulance for the stretcher, but we did not have that kind of time. I pulled her into my arms and made my way through the maze of sheets and out the door. At the bottom of the stairs, I plopped the unconscious female on the stretcher, and we loaded her into the box.

I started an IV and administered oxygen in route to Baylor Medical Center emergency room. At the ER, we rolled past a nurse who yelled over her shoulder, "Room 1, the doctor is waiting." The ER team made quick work and started off to the delivery room with our patient. They were going to take the baby by cesarean section (C-section). A C-section is done by a surgical incision in the abdomen and uterus to allow a baby to be born safely when vaginal birth is not the safest or fastest route.

My partner and I headed back to the box, cleaned up and drove toward the station. A block away from a hopeful nap, the alarm hit again. We left Baylor Medical Center with sirens screaming and lights flashing into downtown Dallas.

In a twenty-four hour shift we made thirty-three runs—total exhaustion was my sidekick.

## My Problem?

Not long after I reported to Station 3, I ran into a chief who mentioned he and his wife had been worried about my problem.

*My problem? What problem?*

Chief said he was discussing me the other night while lying in bed with his wife. Together they had decided that if I were in the shower and got a run, I had a problem. The department had bunkers for the men to step into, and it was okay for men to go shirtless, but I could not go bare-chested.

*Yes, I would say this is a problem. But pillow talk? Really?*

They had decided I could get a jump suit like the paramedics wore at night.

"I was just thinking about a T-shirt, chief," I said.

"Oh no, that will not do! We cannot have wet T-shirts without undergarments at fires. That would be . . . That would be bad," he said without hesitation.

*What do you say to that?*

This chief was an awesome man and a good friend, but thankfully, the bell hit and interrupted our conversation. I was not prepared at the time with an appropriate answer anyhow. He had stated a reality which I soon learned I needed to address. But there was much more to address too. I needed time to think about this and other issues I faced.

Station 3's bathroom had a mirror which ran the length of the bathroom, giving a perfect view of the dressing area and showers from the entry door. Because of this, I would get in the shower, pull the curtain and then undress. I would dry off and completely dress before stepping out from behind the shower curtain. This habit was formed because of a snake-in-the-grass firefighter named Butch. Butch was an old head. Old heads were close to retirement and most proved to be against any change—I was change. I caught Butch peeping in the bathroom door watching my naked reflection in the mirror once. Being reluctant to raise too much fuss, I decided that the best defense was a good offense. I teased Butch in front of the other firefighters calling him a peeping Tom. This was not a good tactical decision on my part, but foresight was not my specialty.

Since Butch strongly felt I did not belong in the department, he began to criticize me. He was quick to point out I could not do the job "as well as a man." Butch was the first person to really push me the wrong way. I had put up with all the agitation and ribbing up to this point fairly well. But Butch's attacks I did not take lightly. He was jeopardizing my job, my convictions, and my destiny with his negative words and attitude. His negativity bred more negativity, and I could see others taking his comments into consideration. They sat quietly thinking and watching both of us.

*Impossible situation!*

Butch had struck a chord, and it brought out the fight in me. It did not feel pretty. At the root of negativity are powerful emotions that make it nearly impossible to consider another person's side. Butch wanted to be in charge. Butch wanted me to believe if he said a pissant could pull a freight train, I was to put the harness on the ant. It was easy for me not to believe or trust Butch.

At one fire, Butch sat on his makeshift throne smoking while watching the rest of us work. I figured I might as well go on the offense, and I took a shot at him. Shamefully, I pointed out his laziness, making sure the others heard me.

Butch's face turned sour, and he thumped his cigarette to the ground while decisively marching toward me hissing, "You think you're so smart. The only reason you're here is the Justice Department forced us to hire you! You will not make it through the end of the year! Women do not belong here! You are taking a job away from a man with a family. Why don't you just give up, go home, and make some babies!"

His cigarette breath drew blood. I felt a slow boil begin inside me. With nothing to say, I stood there shrinking in front of everyone.

*Double impossible!*

Capt. barked us both back to work. I turned, kicked a pile of trash, picked up my hose line, opened the nozzle and sprayed water while choking back crocodile-sized, silent, and shameful tears.

*I will not make it through the end of the year? What does he know that I do not? Is he right? Am I taking away a job from some man that has children to feed? Does my life and future family not count too?*

My certainty was beginning to wane, but I was determined to keep my faith. This man's negative words began to play over again in my mind. By entertaining these ideas, I allowed his words to have credence, simmer inside, and grow. I struggled to forget and move on, but this conflict would resurface in my life many times over. Yet, in the face of this adversity, I was stubborn and just as determined to stay as Butch was to see me go.

*I'm going show him by having a long career. God, are you there? I figure since you're the reason I have this job, nobody can take it from me unless you approve. I really need this job God.*

## Don't Drink the OJ

Station 3 was a great place of gathering, eating, and building camaraderie among firefighters. We had an eating fund in which we all were required to participate. For eight bucks you got three squares a day. We took turns cooking at the station. We rolled dice for dishes. I was good at rolling dice. Rarely did I have to do the dishes. I was good at cards, ping-pong, shooting pool, and rolling dice. After all, I was an athlete.

Whoever was cooking bought the groceries for the shift. There was one slight problem on our shift because we always seemed to forget to purchase orange juice. Not to worry though, the other shifts always had some! We borrowed it from their refrigerator with the intention of replacing it, but it seemed we always forgot. The other shift would come in find their orange juice missing and raise holy heck with us for stealing. Then, it happened one too many times.

It was my turn to ride the box. I saddled up and cleaned up the box. About the time we got the box cleaned and ready to roll, we heard the words, "Soueeeeee, let's eat!" Ferrelli and I raced to the kitchen.

The cook was flipping "bird's nest on the ground" (Texas toast with eggs in the center, served with syrup on the side) on the griddle. We lined up and eagerly waited for the flip into our plate. Over to the table for an individual moment of grace, and then firefighters meticulously encircled their arms around their plate, as if defending their food, and slammed breakfast down as fast as possible. Once the box rolled, the chances were slim-to-none that we would get another full meal for the next twenty-three hours of the shift.

Taking a bite of food, I reached to wash it down with a sip of the orange juice. The juice tasted a little too sweet like it was old or something. The lines on my forehead wrinkled, but I kept eating and drinking because I needed my strength to face a busy shift. There was barely time to eat or rest during a shift on the box.

The bell hit. I took one last bite of my food and grabbed my orange juice glass while running to the box. I opened the door of the ambulance, took one long swig of my juice, sat the glass down on the apparatus room floor and we took off into east Dallas toward a major accident.

At the accident scene, a little old lady seemed confused about what had happened when she was rear-ended. We placed a cervical collar around her neck and then baptized her onto a backboard to protect her from any neck or spinal issues. Once the patient was packaged safely for the ride, we headed toward the hospital. In route to Baylor Medical Center my stomach seemed to roar aloud, and I suddenly felt nauseated.

As we backed into the old underground emergency room at Baylor Medical Center, I wanted to throw up right there in front of my patient.

When Ferrelli opened the back door of the box, I told him I was sick and left him and the paramedic intern to take care of the patient. I spent my time at the hospital in the bathroom throwing up—no use to anyone.

*Check me in! I'm sick too!*

When my stomach finally settled, I surfaced and heard someone in the men's restroom throwing up; it was the paramedic intern. It sounded painful and made me nauseated again. Ferrelli stood smug and smiling.

*He knows something!*

Our intern finally appeared pale and weak. We decided something our cook had made had soured in our stomachs. When we returned to the station, everyone else was also sick with vomiting and diarrhea. Our captain put our station out of service while people chose toilets and threw their guts up.

Ferrelli continued to smile like a possum eating out of a St. Bernard's bowl. By about eleven that morning, we had all recovered and were feeling a little better. My charming partner Ferrelli had zero symptoms!

*He is hiding something about this sudden illness!*

Capt. finally put our station back in service and of course, the bell hit for the box.

After the run I cornered Ferrelli and questioned him until the truth finally came out. The C shift reportedly took a hypodermic needle and shot the orange juice can with ipecac, a solution used to induce vomiting. They wanted to teach us (the A shift) a lesson for stealing their orange juice repeatedly.

*Impossible!*

## Laughing All the Way

Staying wet and wrinkled is the primary job of a rookie at the station. If it was not staying wet, it was something—every day. Sometimes I changed into every clean uniform I had. There were times that all I had left were my workout clothes. I would wear them until all my uniforms dried out. The only thing I could do was laugh. So I laughed. Science shows laughing can be as beneficial to us as exercise.

It was my first opportunity to cook at the fire station. Meticulously, I planned, shopped, cooked, and laid out dinner at Station 3. I spent way too much money for the meal, but I wasn't about to tell the Bubbas about it. I made a fabulous fruit salad, smothered steak with gravy, mashed potatoes, green beans, rolls and banana pudding. Banana pudding was my specialty, so the meringue was browned to perfection with a sprinkle of coconut on the top.

Perfect! I think they are going to love it!

While sweating over the placement of the food filled pans, I worried how my first meal at a fire station would be accepted. The plates were stacked, one on top of the other, forks, knives, and spoons lay out perfectly. I smiled with satisfaction. Taking in a deep cleansing breath, I breathed out slowly, hoping the Bubbas would like my meal.

Placing importance on being accepted, I thought I was accepted right up until one firefighter got a midnight transfer upon my first day at the fire station. That is when I realized it was not acceptable—being a female in the fire service.

*Impossible!*

When dinner was ready, I stepped into the game room at Station 3 and hollered, "Soouueee," the standard dinner bell. Immediately, I heard the engine rev up and pull around near the kitchen door. I stepped back into the kitchen when firefighters came busting in the side door with a hand line used to fight interior house fires. The line was bulging with water and firefighters opened the nozzle and began to wash the food, plates, forks, knives, and spoons, and all my hard work and preparation off the counters. Even the banana pudding was not spared.

The hose lines knocked all the food off onto the floor and then as if power washing the floors, everything was washed out the side door of the fire station. I stood there and wanted to cry until along with the food, plates, pots and pans, I was washed out the door too.

*Double impossible!*

The faces of the men on the end of the hose line said they were just having fun, but my feelings were hurt, not so much over the food, but by not being accepted. This is when Ferrelli who was always respectful and kind, pulled me aside for a little counseling.

"If they like you, they agitate you. If they do not like you, they will not even talk to you."

I trusted Ferrelli, because he was a straight player. I shrugged my shoulders and figured that since they were talking, I was good to go. So I relaxed, gave up being hurt and laughed along with them.

Laughing feels good, and it was right up there with being accepted. We shared in a moment of laughter and our endorphins released, defenses fell, it stirred my soul and suddenly I felt accepted. Joy in the face of challenge is what I learned that day.

*Miracle!*

Firefighters are great at finding ways to let their spirits soar, especially in the face of the impossible. In the face of agitation, harassment and heartache, I found laughter. Laughter has protected me most of my thirty-five-year career. Laughter is another way firefighters live with their *faith on fire*. My friend at the National Speakers Association, Russ Riddle says, "When we laugh, our hero is humbled. When we laugh, we become more human."

Laughing together became a form of unity for me because it was the way firefighters lived their lives. I found that laughing at myself was the best way to be accepted. So, I laughed.

After being washed out of the kitchen and having the counseling session with Ferrelli, we ordered in pizza for dinner. Since I was the cook, I did the ordering.

*Take this!*

Some of the guys got heartburn from the extra bell pepper sprinkled on top. I figured they deserved it, and I laughed myself to sleep.

*Miracle!*

## Fire Department Poop Sheet

One of the funniest things some firefighters would do is write poop sheets. Poop sheets were written about nearly everything throughout my years of service. Poop Sheets covered everything from grooming behaviors to cooking capabilities, and not so surprisingly, a lot of poop sheets were conveniently about me. I just swallowed my pride, smiled and kept putting one foot in front of another.

3 Station Poop Sheet

In one poop sheet, I played the starring roles of the Three Stooges. I was dubbed Larry, Curly, and Moe by one firefighter. This particular poop sheet was written on a paper towel and posted on the bulletin board at the station for everyone to see.

I became good at taking whatever it was dealt my way. I managed through it, most of the time laughing.

## An Agitating Block of What?

"Blessed are we who can laugh at ourselves, for we shall never cease to be amused."

—Sherrie C. Wilson

Walking into Fire Station 3 that day, I had no idea how much fun I would have. I also had no idea how immature we would all act either. They led. I followed. Firefighters love a life filled with drama, and when we did not get it with a high volume of emergency runs, we tended to create it—just for fun.

"Where are my pants?" Pat asked, waking me from a welcomed slumber. I covered my head with my pillow. I was now awake but pretending to sleep, because I knew the location of his pants.

The next time Pat asked the question, he was standing over my bed glaring down at me, wearing only his bunker pants and suspenders.

I yawned. "What pants?" I turned over in my bed so Pat could not see the smile on my face.

*This is going to be fun!*

Pat had agitated me the shift before. He told me I was assigned to pick up all the trash in the gator pit. The gator pit is an atrium in the middle of Station 3.

Years ago, a firefighter brought a pet alligator to Station 3, and it lived in the atrium, lovingly called the gator pit. Firefighters had enjoyed feeding that alligator and watching it rip meat apart. It was fun right up until it became dangerous in size. That is when the chief of the department called in the Dallas Zoo. They took possession of the alligator. The future use of the gator pit was to initiate, harass and agitate rookies.

As the rookie, today would be my formal admission, my rite of passage into the brotHERhood of firefighters. Initiation equaled your first baptism into the fire service, and it is delivered via agitation. Agitation is hard to explain because it is something abnormal. Agitation is an act or process in which you are psychologically and physically irritated until you break or give. The synonyms for agitation include: tumult, storm, unrest, struggle, conflict or disturbance. All of these imply an inner disquiet, a mental tossing to and fro, caused by worry of not knowing that the agitation is coming, or not knowing what they will actually do. This action happens alongside being ignored and given extra duties while shutting you out of conversations.

*Funny, huh?*

When I entered the gator pit and started picking up trash, Pat locked the door with a click and wore a satisfied grin on his face. He walked away and left me there like a sitting duck. It was not until I heard the engine rev up that I had an idea of what was going to happen next.

Shadows moving above me caused me to look up toward the sky. That is when I saw all the men standing on the roof of Station 3 including my captain. They all smiled down at me. It was my official initiation time.

*Good Lord what are they up to now?*

Pat showed up with a nozzle in his hand. A hose line had been laid from the engine, over the roof of Station 3. Pat took aim, pointing the nozzle at me. It was a turkey shoot. It started with a fog spray. I was wet. So what, not a big deal right? Being wet was nothing new. I stayed wet for most of my first year at the fire station.

*It is surprising that I don't have permanently wrinkled skin!*

The stream then changed from a fog to a straight stream—the pressure on the engine panel revved up. The high pressure of the straight stream stung as it smacked at my body. More importantly, the straight stream produced entertainment. This entertainment included me screaming and begging as the high-pressure water slapped me down the walls of the gator pit. I tried to run, to climb the walls, but there was no place to hide. There was nothing I could do except take the agitation and scream.

Water entered my ear at a high pressure. I felt like I was underwater, and all sound became muffled. I turned to protect the injured ear only to have the other ear cleaned out too. I finally squatted into a ball covering my head and ears and played dead. I quit screaming and just stayed in a ball.

The captain finally said, "Enough!" The water stopped.

*Thank God.*

Fearing more agitation, I looked up and they were gone. They put up their toys and left me to dry out. In my mind I had grounds to fight back. But that is not now initiation works. You take it, keep your mouth shut and take it some more. To complain is to violate trust. Initiation is an introduction to the subculture of agitation. Once initiated, agitation becomes the new game.

"So, you got to play their game," Mother always told me. "Watch, learn and play at the same level they do." Mother was talking about business, but I used her wisdom for agitating firefighters.

My father always told me to be quiet and use the element of surprise when you can. He was talking about hunting, but I used his wisdom when paying back agitation at the station too.

Pat met me at the door still wearing his bunkers. I walked out the door of the station. He grabbed me by my arm and yanked me back toward him, looking at me face-to-face. His fiery green eyes pierced mine.

"Where are my pants?" he demanded.

*He could do without the pants; it was the billfold inside he wanted.*

I smiled sheepishly. "Sorry man, I do not know what you're talking about."

*I lied. I am going to do a little shaking and stirring of my own.*

Pat grabbed my arm again and looked at me searching every inch of my face. I smiled but avoided his eye contact. Finally, he let me go.

Dashing to my car, I entered, locked the doors and drove home. Pat was going to have to wait a while for that billfold.

At home, I had my neighbor call Station 3 from his home phone. He told whoever answered the phone to have Pat check the freezer for his pants.

Pat's pants were inside a stew pot filled with water that was now a solid block of ice. The pants had been there all night.

*Finally! I agitated back without getting caught! Yeah baby!*

Sherrie tied to Mimosa tree at Station 3

My next shift at Station 3 was spent tied to a Mimosa tree with plastic restraints used for psycho patients. The Mimosa tree stood proudly in the front yard with me handcuffed nice and snug. The restraints were synched so tight my hands went numb and turned blue. This agitation was a well-coordinated event, because another Bubba smiled deviously while setting the water sprinkler on me. Today, the cook made hamburgers and my personal burger was delivered on a plate, placed on the ground and drowned alongside me. I could not move. All I could do was beg and they walked away laughing and satisfied. I was being taught a strong lesson for trying to retaliate for my initiation. My captain was nowhere in sight, so the Bubbas were in full control.

Suddenly, the bell hit and everybody headed to the apparatus room, leaving me tied to that tree. I thought for sure they would cut me loose to go on an emergency run. I watched the engine, truck, and ambulance all leave the station single file, heading off into downtown on a reported high-rise fire.

*Impossible! Missing an emergency run is grounds for discipline.*

Thinking about how much trouble I could be in, there was nothing left to do but stand there tied to the tree for over an hour with the sprinkler whooshing by periodically. I quit trying to get loose, gave up and fumed, but my heart and mind raced.

*What if a homeless person or gang member comes by? To be exposed in this part of town, tied up and unable to defend myself is not safe. Boy I am going to payback for this! If I could just get loose.*

A Dallas police officer pulled into the parking lot of Station 3. He had come to the station to call in a report. This was before they were equipped with mobile data terminals (computers) inside their vehicles.

*Thank God! Here is my chance to get free!*

He looked at me gravely and sped up when walking toward me with a frown of concern on his face. He snapped open his knife to cut me loose and rescue me. With uneasiness in his voice, he asked, "What happened?"

"Agitation," I explained.

"Agitation?"he questioned.

Once I fully explained agitation to him, he smiled, snapped his knife closed, and turned to walk off, leaving me tied up. He was not going to get involved in fire department games.

*Double impossible!*

Without an ounce of hesitation, my eyes filled with saucer-sized tears.

"My hands are aching and they have turned blue. What if a homeless man or gang member comes by? I am helpless to defend myself. Please help me! Please!"

He thought about it for a moment. After all, I had been bound and held against my will. I was in a state of extreme arousal, excited, tense, confused, afraid and begging. He shook his head in disgust, snapped open his pocket knife and cut me loose.

*Finally, someone had mercy on me—miracle.*

All I know was Pat went to bed that night with his pants on. It was not long that I heard him get out of the bed. He was dusting himself off. He was obviously aggravated and grumbled at a low level in the dark. I lay in my bed trying not to laugh out loud. I covered my head with a pillow and then the bell hit. We both darted toward the ambulance.

When we got in the box, Pat looked like a ghost. He was covered with flour from head to toe. I laughed so hard, I almost peed my pants. It was funny to hear him tell the patient about flour falling on his head at a fire.

We transported our patient to Parkland Memorial Hospital. Ever the lady's man with all the nurses, Pat now had a lot of explaining to do.

"DO NOT ASK," was his standard answer.

Winking at the nurses questioning Pat, I stood smug, feeling successful for a change.

Pat was not a happy camper, but he finally called a truce and gave up agitating me. Out of the hundreds of times I was agitated, this one payback was utterly rewarding and memorable. Even Pat laughed about it later—after he took a shower at about three a.m., which was not until after three more emergency runs.

Dedication: This story is dedicated to all those that influence and inspire others through humor. Humor, laughter and teasing provided not only a source of joy, but it kept me grounded in humility.

# Chapter 3

---

# STEADY BURNING PHASE

Definition: The stage of a fire when sufficient oxygen and fuel are available for fire growth and open burning to a point of total involvement of fire with contents.

## The Marlboro Man

From 1954-1999, the Marlboro Man, a ruggedly handsome cowboy, was used in tobacco advertising campaigns for Marlboro cigarettes. Scott looked like the Marlboro Man: a body like a steal trap, the mustache and heavy brows, the black cowboy hat and those tight, black jeans he wore into the station. I felt like I needed to pray after watching him waltz into the station every shift though. Scott was off limits. He was married and he also smoked, both were on my do-not-date list. But there was something unique about this man—he was just plain nice. Nice to talk to, work with, and most importantly, Scott protected me when I really needed it, not once, but twice.

Back in the late 70s, we had a great engine, but it had its fair share of problems. When our driver-engineer could not fix it, we called the shop. The guy driving the maintenance truck was nice enough, but he could not hit the side of a barn with a baseball when standing ten feet away. Plus he was more interested in eating our cutback (leftovers) than he was fixing our engine. We knew he would make us swap out all our equipment onto a different engine that probably was not as safe as ours was. It always cost time and a lot of work to take every piece of equipment off our engine and put it on the loaner engine. The only loaner engine available that day was an old red training engine with an open cab just like in children's story books: the members stood up on the tail board.

It was freezing outside when the bell hit. I pulled on my 3/4 boots and put my arm into one side of my coat. The driver-engineer started the engine and popped the clutch at the very moment I let go of the safety bar, attempting to put my other arm in the other side of the coat. The engine jerked forward. I started falling backwards and would have cracked open the concrete floor with my head had Scott not grabbed the neck of my coat and pulled me safely to him.

*Miracle!*

We took off into downtown Dallas. The first bump we hit in the road, my feet lifted off the tailboard and the tips of my toes barely held on. Again, I was pulled to safety and told, "Bend your knees." They act as a cushion for the bumps.

*Double miracle!*

I gripped the safety rail tighter and prayed. I prayed we did not have another run the rest of the shift. I would rather face the Dallas Knife and Gun Club on a Saturday night blow-out than ride the tailboard of an open cab engine going code 3 with a firefighter nicknamed Bam-Bam driving.

The National Fire Protection Association (NFPA) writes the standards for the fire service. The 1992 edition of NFPA 1901 called for fully enclosed cabs or open jump seats and officially ended the riding of tailboards.

*Triple miracle!*

One great thing I remember at Station 3 was that the Bubbas protected me. They dug down and did the right thing, even though some of them did not believe I belonged there. I was their sister in the fire service and although they agitated me, humped my leg, and harassed me on a regular basis, they protected me. Most importantly, the men at Station 3 had joy and an amazing faith-on-fire winning attitude! We loved our jobs, and for the most part we loved each other, and it was a miracle of a job.

## Lead Smelter

I had never heard of a lead smelter with one exception. The news media had reported about a west Dallas neighborhood next to a smelter and a lot of people were getting sick from lead poisoning. Some families received some kind of settlement for medical expenses due to illness.

"Let's go now on a one-alarm lead smelter fire, Dawson and Jefferies."

When riding Engine 3 up and over the bridge into south Dallas, I could see smoke was pouring out of the building.

*We got one!*

We stretched a line and went inside the one story warehouse structure with powdery grey smoke rolling out, leaving a metallic taste to the air. We hurried up inside the structure and found a huge furnace bubbling with an angry silver liquid material. The furnace was the size of a small home, and its mouth dripped and spit blobs of liquid in every direction. The radiant heat from the out-of-control furnace fire caught wooden pallets stacked nearby on fire.

Suddenly, my line filled with water, and I drew down on the furnace and started to open the nozzle.

My captain quickly ordered, "Sherrie, only hit the pallets, and do not aim at the furnace!"

I shrugged my shoulders and did as instructed hitting only the burning wooden pallets. We stood there a long time watching the liquid calm and cool. I was curious about what the metal was used for and why it did not mix with water.

When picking up my hose line, I asked Capt., "Why didn't we put the water directly on the furnace?"

"It would have spit lead back at you and boiled you alive, girl," he said jokingly.

*Seriously, I almost put water on that smelter.*

I got a miracle that day in the form of an officer who was good at direction and reading the uneducated moves of a rookie. I felt sick for a little while and thought about what it would be like to have my skin melting off at this very moment. Would I be screaming? Would the pain be intolerable? What would the firefighters think of a female who got herself hurt at the very beginning of her career? Would some of them be glad that I had learned my lesson for daring to step into a man's world?

Smelting is a form of extraction that uses heat and a chemical-reducing agent to change the oxidation state of metal ore. Its purpose is to remove any accompanying impurities.

Like the lead smelter, my life would be heated, boiled, stirred, and an extraction would need to take place. The boil started slow and grew over the years, but it was not a lead smelter, it was a refiner's fire that would work to change my life.

## Five Minutes with the Evil Runt

The report stated: Third day—locked in a closet.

A hint of light in the crack at the top of the door was her only ray of hope for days. Around 5:30 pm, he entered their home. This is where he kept everything he owned. He owned her.

He opened the refrigerator door, grabbed a beer and turned on the television. Soon the refrigerator door opened again and again and again. Not a good sign. Beer dulled his sense of fairness. Beer made him forget about love. Beer made him act out. Beer equaled a beating.

*Impossible situation!*

She had wrestled out of her restraints so she was ready and waiting. When he finally decided it was time for another beating, he reached to open the door where he kept his prized possession. He was surprised when she kicked it open with all her might. The door met his chin. He stumbled backwards and fell. He lay still, bleeding.

When she dashed for freedom, he jolted up and grabbed her from behind, his arm around her neck. Everything went dark. Her ninety-eight pounds hit the ground. He had won, again. Thinking he had strangled her unconscious, he stormed toward the garage.

She rolled onto her stomach and pushed herself up, willing herself to get out. He was going to kill her. He'd promised it for years. She steadied herself against a table and attempted to focus. He rushed toward her, a sharpened lawn mower blade in hand.

A spark of energy shot through her as she ran. She raced toward the door and stepped through the threshold just as he swung and missed. She felt the hard cold steel whiz by the back of her neck. She sped up. Running down the steps, she looked everywhere for anyone or anything that could protect her. No open doors begged her to enter and be safe. No place to hide.

The screaming and cursing from behind kept her darting back-and-forth to avoid his vicious stabs. The faster she ran, the madder he got. He was gaining ground. Out of breath, she stopped on the opposite side of the merry-go-round and faced her attacker. He stopped, giving her a reprieve but continued to curse. Foul words poured from his mouth, revealing his heart. She was dead!

Neighbors came out to watch the ruckus then jerked inside after witnessing the violence and drama.

He approached slowly and smiled. She stumbled and fell. He began swinging the blade of the lawn mower like it was an ax. Hate poured from his heart and flowed down his arms as he chopped at her body, and she screamed from the pit of her being with pain. He hit the back of her head with the flat of the blade. She saw dark. Then he hit her in the back, and it cut through to her lung, air gushed out. He slammed at her body like a maniac.

She lay still, battered and bruised. In hate, he swung at his property, knowing he could do as he wished. In his mind, there were no rules.

Neighbors had called the police.

We got the call as an aggravated assault in the park. Normally we beat the police to incidents like this, but thankfully central station was only a few blocks away. The place was swarming with police when we arrived.

We pulled up as the police officers jerked him off her. One officer took the blade away while another police officer wrestled him face-to-the-ground and handcuffed him. It took a slew of officers to put the angry man in the back seat of the squad car.

She lay unconscious, barely breathing. We made quick work of her injuries. The lawn mower blade lacerations were on her head, neck and back. She had curled into a ball trying to protect herself from the monster. The heaviness of the blade caused a multitude of blunt trauma injuries as well as the penetrating wound in her back, which had punctured her lung. The wound sucked in outside air with every shallow breath she took and the extra air was tightening down on her lungs like a vice grip. Her breathing got faster and harder.

We controlled bleeding, slapped a 4 x 4 dressing covered with Vaseline on her sucking chest wound and immobilized her C Spine. We did not have the fancy dressings like we do today.

It was time to take off for the hospital and my turn to drive. I closed the back door of the box and paused for a split second to look at the face of the animal sitting in the squad car. He seemed to be talking to himself. Maybe he was finally realizing what he had done. Maybe it had hit him like a lawn mower blade that this was his last time to do this to anyone outside the penitentiary.

A light was on in the squad car and he looked back at me with a snarl. I felt a shiver run across my body and then my teeth clenched. He had the face of evil, but he was a runt of a guy. The only thing that made him big was his ego. I walked to the front of the box whispering under my breath and squeezing both hands into a fist.

*God, give me just five minutes with this evil runt!*

Shaking the anger from my mind, I released the emergency brake and took off with lights and sirens for Parkland Memorial Hospital. In route, I wiped silent and sorrowful tears from my cheeks and prayed for the limp body in the back of my ambulance. Driving through traffic, my eyes continued to swell, and I fought it until finally, I cried. Crying releases the stress, but I cannot let anyone see me cry. I do not usually cry. Do not ask me why; I just cannot. The guys do not cry, so I do not cry either. Prior to Critical Incident Stress Management training, crying was seen as weak.

*Just five minutes with the evil runt, God!*

You question God, and you tell him you do not like it. You wish for revenge, but you cannot repay evil with evil. You cannot get involved. The frustration swells into your throat and hovers. Finally, you cry. Then you pray for the patient and for forgiveness.

*My miracle came tonight dressed in tears of forgiveness.*

Light always overcomes darkness. This woman is now in the light.


Dedication: This story is dedicated to anyone who has suffered abuse in life. Know that your emergency services personnel hurt through silent tears.

## The Wives

Being six foot tall and stronger than your average female, in college I was the one on the bottom of the cheerleading team holding up and flipping the tiny girls. When I was not cheerleading, I was playing basketball. I had been a worthy adversary to many a female on the basketball court. Today the court had changed, but the opponent remained the same. (Women, the wives, not the men as previously thought.)

Just before I reported to Station 3, I received a letter addressed from a group called Women United. The unsigned letter said:

"Sherrie, how very tragic you didn't have parents who taught you right and wrong! It is a sin for you to be living with other women's husbands. It is a sin for you to be turning our fire houses into whore houses. May God forgive you."

Sherrie:

How very tragic that you didn't have parents who taught you right and wrong!

It is a sin for you to be living with other women's husbands It is a sin for you to be turning our fire-houses into whore houses May God forgive you.

Women United
P.O. Box 671
Houston, Texas
77000

Fire Cadet Sherri Clark
% Dallas Fire Department
Dallas, Texas
75201

Whoever wrote this did not know me, never met me, and had no idea how I was raised. I did have parents teach me right from wrong—I just wanted a *job*. I thought this was some kind of sick-minded person, but people's beliefs are powerful and closed minds are like mine fields—a difficult place to navigate safely.

When I arrived at Station 3, one firefighter's wife was upset over me being at the station; he ended up on a midnight transfer. The funny thing is, his marriage to her did not last even with him in a different fire station. Some wives did not like me being at the station, but most were kind, and I appreciated their support. However, there was one harsh exception.

One particularly severe looking female with heavy make-up came into the station to use the phone. She was wearing a tight pair of red jeans that looked like she had been melted and poured in them. She had donned red cowboy boots and a matching red cowboy cut shirt with the sleeves cut off at the shoulder. She had the reddest orange hair I had ever seen in my life and one of those flamboyant rat-it-up, tease-it-up, and bitch-it-out hairdos. This is what we call "big hair" in Texas. And in Texas, everything is bigger anyway. She reeked of heavy perfume mixed with the odor of cigarettes, and her lips were wrinkled in a pooch fashion from having sucked on cigarettes for most of her adult life.

As I walked into the watch room, I noticed her with her back to me, quietly whispering to one of the firefighters. The female turned and walked by me toward the phone booths, and my eyes began to water because her perfume was so heavy. Although we were not introduced, I felt something sinister about her. I cannot really explain it, but something wicked hung invisibly around her. A chill crossed my body, and I promptly left the room.

Once the female finished her call and departed, I overhead some of the guys talking. She not only looked harsh, she was a stripper who was known for over-dosing on alcohol.

One of the rookie assignments was to answer the station telephone while everyone else relaxed and watched TV. Tonight was no different: The phone rang, and I answered.

"Station 3, how may I help you?"

Expletive after expletive were screamed through the phone. It was a garbled, drunken tirade on the other end of the line.

"Excuse me," I said not understanding.

"You heard me you @$#%&, I am coming up there and kicking your @#%," said the slurred words. It was a female voice at the other end of the line.

*This must be a wrong number?*

Attempting to clarify, I said, "I am sorry ma'am, you got Dallas Fire Station 3."

"I know who the @#$& I called. You stupid @#$&*, I am talking to you! You're the stupid @#$& that is sleeping with my husband. I'm going to kill you," the hateful words slurred together and dripped with sarcasm.

*This person had plum drunk herself silly.*

People love to make up stories, and they love drama.

*God love 'em!*

This was a little of both. I absolutely did not sleep with anyone at the station. I did sleep in the same bedroom as all the other firefighters, but in my own cubbyhole and bed.

I hung up the phone, went to my lieutenant and reported the conversation. The lieutenant reported the call to the captain.

Soon after, the phone rang again. The captain answered this time, and it was the same caller. I could hear her disgusting remarks through the phone. Soon I was told it was the same female who visited the station earlier today. She came to the station to check me out and because she found me to be a decent, attractive, female, she went home, drank herself stupid and decided I was a problem. Turns out she was the wife of one of my co-workers.

I overheard the captain tell her, "No, do not come up here. I have already called the police and if you come, you will be arrested."

Some of the guys cornered me and told me about the Mrs. She was a full time stripper that danced with a snake in one of the strip clubs on

Industrial Boulevard. Supposedly, she was a part time drug addict too, not to mention the obvious alcohol problem.

*God, she is impossible!*

My coworker was a nice guy at the station, but his face proved otherwise. One big scar ran from the corner of his mouth down one side of his chin. Station gossip told daring stories of a man who would drink and fight just for fun. One firefighter told me that when this couple drank together, they were known for clearing out bars by fighting together, too.

*God, she is double impossible!*

One of the firefighters said, "We used to go out with them, but they are both too wild. My wife refused to tolerate how they behaved."

One Bubba told me that when riding Ambulance 703 with my co-worker, another ambulance crew riding 711 called them by radio requesting a meeting at an intersection near the edge of both districts. Ambulance 711 had picked up the stripper wife, and she was extremely drunk and belligerent. Her husband, my coworker, purportedly crawled up inside 711 and carried his wife out like a sack of potatoes. He flung her into 703, crawled up inside the box with her and slammed the door behind himself. The medics standing outside the ambulance heard him slap his wife several times. Eventually they took her back to Station 3 and loaded her up in his car and he took her home.

*The Bubbas never let me ride with this co-worker. Now I know why. They were protecting me.*

Having heard enough of the conversation, I walked away. I tried to remain calm and act disinterested. Underneath I was worried, and a dreadful fear percolated through my heart.

My captain and lieutenant tried to keep me in one room where they could keep an eye on me, but I began to pace around the station like a cat cornered by a mountain lion.

*Was she really coming up here? People will do anything when jacked up on drugs and alcohol. This female knew something about her husband I did not want to know!*

When the wife's calls had come into the station, her husband, my co-worker, was on an emergency run. When he returned, I overhead the captain telling him what had gone down. Captain was mad because he had to put the entire station out of service due to this threat. My co-worker was given an hour off to go home and talk to his wife.

"Get her under control," my captain ordered! The captain was firm and added, "I will not tolerate anyone threatening one of my men, ah, I mean my crew."

*How about my female? Well, even that sounds wrong.*

"Now tell your wife if she does this again that your job is in jeopardy," he barked.

"Yes sir," was the reply from my co-worker.

To end the episode, I was ordered to go to bed like a school-aged child and not come out of the bedroom no matter what. I walked into the bedroom, and I overheard the lieutenant tell the Bubbas to, "Lock up and hunker down. She told the captain that she was on her way." Bubbas were assigned to lock and guard every door to the station.

The belief appeared to be that she was capable of following through on her threat. One firefighter trying to console me said, "When my wife and I went out with this couple, she made it known she carries a gun."

*A gun? Would she really use it? What would make her hate me? I felt an impossible darkness surround me.*

A call was made to my chief, and I am sure his little round face turned wine red. His face always turned the color of merlot when it came to anything regarding his assigned female.

*Double impossible. I hadn't seen this much drama on the ambulance, and now I was in the middle of it all.*

As I lay in the bed, I swallowed hard. My throat was dry. I felt an intense anguish and a sense of loneliness not only for myself but for this woman too.

*What is her story? What happened to her to cause her life to be like this?*

Immediately, I overheard the captain and lieutenant talking. My coworker had found his wife one block away from Station 3, and she had the gun in her possession, but everything was now under control.

*Really?*

It wasn't until Capt. got on the radio and put us back in service did I really believe she had been stopped.

*Thank you God for this miracle!*

The men did not tease me about her threats. As a matter of fact, I do not remember talking with them after that night about this incident.

*Double miracle!*

I never heard from her again.

A few years after this, after my coworker had retired, his wife reportedly committed suicide. The firefighter telling me the story said, "She was a tormented soul. I think the alcohol and drugs finally got to her."

Amazingly in the midst of all the racing heart, overwhelming fear and uncivilized threats, I knew those firefighters were there to defend me.

*Triple miracle!*

Dedication: This story is dedicated to anyone who has suffered with drug or alcohol use.

## Thank You, Big Mamma

Big Mamma was—well, she was just big. Big mama was sweet, round, and jiggly. She had white teeth, dark brown eyes, chocolate colored skin and a six-foot-tall personality. The paramedics riding 703 knew her well. We got calls from her at times, mostly breathing difficulty. Today she just wanted her blood pressure checked. Big Mamma also told me her water heater had gone out. I looked up at my partner Ferrelli and nodded my head toward the water heater. Ferrelli, ever the gentleman, got down on his knees and lit the pilot light to the heater. Big Mama reached for me and gave me a big hug. She smelled of lavender.

*I love the smell of lavender.*

Big Mamma thanked us and tried to pass out homemade cookies. We both declined, thanking her with a smile and headed back to Station 3.

Big Mamma's son was a known drug addict—heroin. He had recently been released from jail and moved back with her into the small apartment in the Roseland town home projects, which lay under the east shadow of downtown Dallas. When we pulled up to take care of Big Mamma, her son and his buddies were spending their workday out front of the housing projects on a park bench doing absolutely nothing. I noticed her son did not come to check on his mother when we arrived. He did however, point at me and a couple of his friends laughed about something he said.

*Whatever?*

The dudes were wearing red—normal colors for members of the gang in in this part of town. Red bandanas were mostly tied around their head or necks. It was always a guessing game for us as to the honor our clients lived with.

When we left Big Momma's house, these gangsters made some lewd gestures toward us. I knew they were directed at me, but I just shrugged my shoulders, and we drove away. Ferrelli and I talked about how they looked like trouble, but we did not think we would see them again.

*Dunderheads.*

Midnight, the bell hit. We had just laid down from a punishing day, racking up fifteen runs in the first seventeen hours of the shift. We heaved our exhausted bodies and sleepy eyes toward the box and prepared for more. I knew the address—it was Big Mamma's. I would go in, be greeted with a hug and then take her blood pressure, assess her breathing and probably take her on to Parkland Memorial Hospital if her congestive heart failure was causing increased breathing difficulty or unusual swelling in her ankles.

We entered Big Mamma's house. She was nowhere in sight, but the thugs and her dopey son who were present earlier on that park bench were here.

*Where is Big Mamma?*

Her son and his buddies, about eight total, were sitting around the room looking like it was party time.

Big Mamma's son sat in her recliner and pretended to be sick surrounded by his smirking cronies. His buddies made some weird faces between one another and used hand signals I did not understand.

"I do not feel good," the son said while holding his belly with one arm. His face said otherwise. My gut did not actually feel that good either, and my forehead broke out in a sweat.

*Hmm . . . something is not right here.*

I knelt down in front of my patient to assess his vital signs. As I took a knee, everyone in the room laughed out loud. One guy made a lewd gesture toward me and seemed to be egging on the leader.

*What is going on?*

While wrinkling my brow, I started to get up, but something stopped me—a sudden confusion or disbelief, I am not sure. I shook my head wishing it away, but did not take my eyes off the leader.

I glanced back at Ferrelli standing in the door way. He had a radio in one hand—taking notes with the other. Suddenly, he stopped writing and slowly backed out the door. He would not make eye contact with me.

*Where's he going? Impossible!*

Eye contact might have triggered an emotional response—a sign of weakness. Any sign of weakness, and it would all be over for both of us.

Alarm caused my breath to quicken. I was in the crosshairs of some eleventh hour scheme by a drug addict.

*God, get me out of here!*

Still on my knees, I finished the blood pressure and started asking questions, pretending not to notice the signs of trouble. I was like a duck on the water all smooth and calm on the outside, but my mind was paddling like crazy underneath. I was not getting reasonable answers to the medical questions, and the son appeared to be playing possum. The sneers on their faces reeked of trouble, and I was way past being tolerant. I glared defiantly at Big Mamma's son and started to give him a piece of my mind—something stopped me again.

The room full of troublemakers kept looking at one another then back at me, as if deciding which one would strike first.

*They are chicken! Messing with a sworn officer is a felony.*

When debating whether to bolt, curiosity and something else I cannot not explain, kept stopping me—it was an unusual calm that spread its wings and hovered over me.

*I have got a job to do. What if he is really sick? Maybe I am reading this wrong.*

Big Mamma's son eyes glazed over with hate and his huge arms began to reach toward me ready to pounce. I recoiled leaning backwards.

*Oh, God, no!—Wait a minute, I smell lavender!*

Then I heard my last minute miracle on the way. The faces in the room shifted from games to grief. They were stopped in their tracks. I had heard her shuffle before.

*Miracle!*

Big Mamma came jiggling down the stairs in that familiar shuffle of hers. She was wearing a yellow muumuu with pink rollers placed strategically around her head and furry pink bathroom slippers. I thought something odd when I entered the apartment, but I could not put my finger on it. With congestive heart failure, Big Mama usually slept in the recliner downstairs—it made it easier for her to breathe.

Big Mamma took one look in the room and in a loud controlling voice yelled, "What ya bad boys up to? I'm gonna beat the tar out o' ya, son!"

The grown men shrugged their shoulders innocently, and their palms went face up in defeat. My palms broke out in a chilly sweat as I rose hastily to my feet.

Big Mamma chastised her adult child in front of me. "Don'ya be messin' with my fraends!" She waved at me to gather my things and get out with the command presence of chief.

"They take care o' me, son! Ya can't keep livin'dis way boy!" she said, hollering, and then nodded in my direction to get out. "Don' ya worry I will take care o' dese boys."

Big Mamma waddled over and started swinging and slapping in every direction except mine. Hands went up to protect themselves, but no one ran from her—she meant business!

Slinging everything into my equipment bag, I high-tailed it outside looking for my partner and left Big Mamma tending to her bad boy business. Big Mamma was still inside screaming at the top of her lungs when I found Ferrelli.

Frogging Ferrelli in the arm I said, "Why did you leave me in there all by myself? I hate to think of what could have happened."

Ferrelli explained that he feared he could not take all the guys on at once and he sensed we were both in trouble. He stepped out to call police with an "assist officer" call. This call gets us police back-up, code 3, lights and sirens. In the distance I heard sirens, and it was not long till police started pulling up at the scene with lights flashing. The police units arriving from all sides lit up the darkened government housing apartments referred to as the Projects. I felt like I was in a movie scene for a moment. The entire housing project was shrouded in red and blue flashing lights with white headlights pointing toward Ferrelli and me.

According to Big Mamma, I was in trouble and she told the police on her son and she sided with us.

*He reached for me, but he never laid a hand on me. God you are so good!*

After answering questions by the police, I swallowed hard and turned walking toward the box. Once I was alone in the box I sat quietly.

*Thank you God for a partner that could read this situation and acted on by behalf. Thank you for Big Mama, but most importantly, thank you for answering my prayer and keeping me safe!*

A miracle—just for me? Thankful tears swelled in my eyes, but I wiped them quickly not wanting anyone to think I was weak.

Big Mamma and Ferrelli stepped up, both acting to protect me. I appreciated their effort, but when I was on my knees in front of those troublemakers, it was not them I was talking to. I knew my protection came from God above.

Big Mamma's wayward son continued to be a disappointment. The next time we went to see Big Mamma; she cried a river of tears into my shoulder because that son of hers beat her to the grave—overdosing on heroin. This time I hugged her, and she held on to me tightly. She loved her son, but he had gotten to be too much, and it never crossed his mind to be obedient.

Once Big Mamma was alone, Ferrelli and I checked on her periodically; she had become our Big Mamma too. I finally gave in and ate some of her cookies, because she did not have anybody else to make them for. Whenever we were called to the Projects, Big Mamma greeted us with a hug and helped direct us to the right apartment. Her joy was in helping us and hugging me.

The last time I saw Big Mamma, her neighbor had found her and called 911. We arrived and the neighbor pointed worriedly at Big Mamma's door saying she was not breathing. I entered her apartment and found her in her recliner—she was dead and at peace. Her once jiggling body was now stiff as a board. There was nothing to do but touch her hand, close her eyes, and say a prayer of thanks to God for putting her in my life. Big Mamma was precious.

*No more hugs.*

Silent tears fell as she was a precious, loving and honorable woman in my eyes.

Big Mamma was tough as tar, but her heart was white as freshly spun silk, and she reached out and helped me when I faced the impossible.

*She was a miracle to me. We were different as night and day but she taught me something about love. Love creates unity. Love creates miracles. I loved Big Mamma.*

Big Mamma was one of many residents I interacted with in my years of service. Never did I feel more like I was in the right place at the right time than when I was serving the citizens of Dallas aside the men and women of the Dallas Fire Department.

During emergencies, the color of skin, ethnic backgrounds, wealth and education do not matter. In the face of many impossible situations, unity is where miracles are found.

*The first ingredient of this miracle was most certainly an impossible situation.*

Dedication: This story is dedicated to all the citizens of Dallas, Texas. You trusted me with your life, and I learned everyday while serving you. My life is rich with an array of family and friends whom I will never forget.

## Rescue Me

Thick black smoke puffed from the building in the southeast part of downtown Dallas. It was built back in the 1930s, and we called it Main Street USA construction. The red brick building was only two stories high and had served many useful purposes over its life. It was now serving as offices on the second floor with a small warehouse on the first floor.

When we arrived, we all rushed the door like a bunch of little puppies trying to get to the same food bowl. We made for a funny sight as we could not all fit through the door at the same time. I was elbowed and pushed aside and was one of the last few to enter the building.

When I finally entered the smoke-filled building, I headed up the stairwell toward the fire on the second floor following the same path all the others had taken. I ran the first few steps and hit a landing, then turned to finish my ascent.

*Bam! Free falling.*

Suddenly, I dropped down several feet, only stopping when my butt wedged between the broken boards of the damaged landing. The building was dark and the few firefighters following me up the steps stumbled over me, but they kept going toward the fire. Firefighters thought I had just tripped and passing me up was part of the game we play. Firefighters never want to be last.

Finally, the last firefighter up the stairs sensed something was wrong. He hesitated and then realized that I had fallen through the landing. It did not take us long to understand I was also pinned. The firefighter backed down a step and pulled me toward him. He could not budge me an inch. I was wedged between the splintered boards and each tug took a bite out of my hip.

*Impossible situation!*

Bubba radioed for help and almost immediately firefighters appeared and surrounded me.

*I was expecting angels and they came dressed in bunker gear. Miracle!*

There was not much left of the landing, so some firefighters were standing on steps below me and some were standing on steps above me. Needless to say, we were all riding a timeworn stairwell that could give way any minute. There was still fire roaring above us on the second floor, and smoke was banking down the stairwell.

*God, hurry this miracle a little. I'm not doubting—just saying.*

In order to pull me out, I would have to be lifted vertically, but there was no place to stand to pull me up vertically. There were muffled groans and determined spirits, but together as a team they all lifted, pulled, and tugged—nothing.

The rickety stairwell started to sway with some of the firefighters above. They held on, and the stairwell stopped swaying. Determined, they tugged again, this time upwardly. The wood pinched my hips and my knee twisted during the fall. Bubbas shuffled again for position, but with a final jerk, they finally pulled me up and out of the dark hole.

*Double miracle!*

This was the first of several times I was carried to the ambulance. My friend Hank was the paramedic in charge that day. Hank looked with concern in his eyes, but once he assessed me, he settled down. A few scratches, bruises, a twisted knee and ankle which is minor compared to what could have happened had I had fallen all the way through into the next floor or basement. I was transported to Baylor Medical Center just east of downtown. It was protocol. I got a few shifts off to recover mainly for my injured knee.

It was a surprise to the Bubbas when I returned to work a few shifts later. There were bets going down as to whether or not an injury would do me in.

"She's baaaack," I heard one of them say to another.

Yes, I was back, not only from the injury, but I became more determined than ever to finish what I started and complete my career. This was not the only time I was injured.

If someone needs time off for a vacation or for a family reunion, we just worked for each other—we called this subbing. While subbing for a Bubba on the B-shift, I caught a fire in south Dallas.

Once a fire is out firefighters go around hitting the hot spots—places where fire might be buried in a wall or ceiling. Fire was falling down from the old shiplap ceiling: old wooden slats used prior to the widely-available sheet rock used today. I tugged hard on the shiplap, and it did not budge. I doubled my efforts and yanked with everything I had and suddenly a 2x6 wood board came down and knocked me in the head.

Walking around in circles and feeling for a moment like I was in a cartoon with birds tweeting above my head, the B-shift captain now eyeing me said, "Are you okay?"

"I think so," was my response.

*I am a rookie, I can't tell him I am hurt, or they will fire me for sure. I've already hurt my knee.*

Several months later my neck was really bothering me.

For the next few years I was a regular visitor to the chiropractic school in Dallas that gave discounts to police and fire. The x-ray of my neck showed a girl who should not be doing any heavy lifting and certainly not firefighting.

While sitting in a church service on a Wednesday night, pastor John Kershaw at Christian World Church, pointed at me saying, "Come here young lady, God is going to heal your neck."

*How does he know about my neck? I never told anyone.*

Pastor Kershaw laid hands on me and said, "In the name of Jesus, heal this neck."

*God, only you knew about my neck.*

The pastor's touch released a warm feeling starting at my head, and it ran the length of my spine. I fought fire for another thirty years.

*Miracle!*

Not only had God given me this job, he helped me continue my career by doing a supernatural miracle just for me. He healed my neck!

In addition, God gave me co-workers who delivered miracles of the most ordinary kind, but they were miracles just the same. I felt like I had more brothers, dads, uncles, and grandpas a girl could ever want. They stepped up to protect me again and again. That said, I couldn't say the same for the Duke.

Dedication: This story is dedicated to the brotHERhood in the Fire and EMS services who reached down and lifted another in their time of need.

# Chapter 4

# FLAME SPREAD PHASE

Definition: Presence of superheated air is one of the reasons firefighters are taught to keep low and use protective breathing equipment. One breath can sear the lungs.

## The Duke

Swinging from one station to another was what firefighters did in order to balance manpower across the city. Rookies didn't swing until they had completed ten shifts. It was my first time to swing.

When the call came into the station to swing a man to Station 19, I heard someone snicker, "The chief doesn't know it is her time to swing and nobody is going to tell him. They are swinging her to Station 19!"

Back in the late 1970s, Station 19 was notorious for everything short of criminal behavior. It was rumored to be a haven for outlaw firefighters, especially one named the Duke.

The Duke's cold black hair reeked of dye. He wore large, flashy gold rings on each hand, and his big, broad shoulders shadowed the beer belly that hung over his belt. The pointed black cowboy boots he wore with his fire department uniform chimed "illegal" with regard to the department's rules and regulations manual. He drove a Texas-sized

Cadillac and crowned himself with a black cowboy hat when off-duty. Reportedly, he spent a lot time at local watering holes with women who adored him.

On this day he tried to look youthful and cool in front of me. I think he saw himself as the quintessential lady's man. His leathery skin, along with every other inauthentic thing about him, just made me think *old*.

He welcomed me into the fire station while licking his lips. He methodically rubbed his chin as though putting together a plan. He whispered flirtatious comments about my tall, lean, slender body. He raised his eyes toward heaven and thanked God for his visual gift. He hoped to impress me when he flashed a smile and a wink. I returned the smile and walked out of the room to put my gear on the engine.

Arriving at Station 19, I was ready to take on the world for the first time outside of Station 3. I was unaware of this station's history or the firefighters working here. Once my chief got wind that I had swung to Station 19 and realized the station captain was off on a vacation day, he called in a panic. He understood that I was now amid the real outlaws of the department and without any supervision.

My chief ordered the lieutenant at Station 19 to swing a man to Station 17, the chief's house. The lieutenant turned to me and started to speak, but the Duke stepped up and intervened, whispering something. Had it not been for the bars on the lieutenant's collar, it would have been difficult to distinguish who was in charge, the lieutenant or the Duke?

The Duke had a commanding presence, and it was clear he had power. Driver-engineers are like middle management in the fire station. If the officer was off duty the driver-engineer stepped up and ran things. The Duke knew the chief wanted me swung back to his station so he could keep an eye on me, but the Duke convinced the lieutenant that he was ordered to swing a *man*, not a *woman*.

Needless to say, the chief was not happy when one of the male firefighters from Station 19 showed up at his station. He clearly wanted me there, but somewhere in backroom conversations between the chief and the lieutenant, I ended up staying at Station 19 for the entire shift.

I now belonged to the Duke for the next twenty-four hours. I was his—all his.

*Like a duck on a June bug.*

After a cup of coffee and some small talk, the Duke took it upon himself to introduce me to everyone at the station. He guided me around with his hand at my back. He moved me like he would a woman on the dance floor. I broke free and went into the telephone booth pretending to make a call, just to be free of the Duke's smell and touch. I wondered what it was going to take to successfully navigate through the shift.

The Duke resembled an old-time country-western singer including his raven black hair and deep, raspy, smoke-filled voice. Smoke mixed with heavy, sweet cologne permeated the space around him, and he reeked with infidelity. He was known for playfully grabbing and pawing at other firefighter's wives and girlfriends. He did the same with me without permission. This was a man who clearly ruled the roost in his home—and this station was his home. His behavior was something more closely related to a dog with a bone, and I felt gnawed upon. Unsure of what to do, I managed to giggle like a schoolgirl and pull away every time I was pawed or grabbed.

*Impossible! This never happened at Station 3. What do I do now?*

Hunkering down in the restroom much longer than necessary, I then heard him call, "Here little lady, let me get you another cup of coffee. What does the little lady want me to cook for breakfast?"

*Is this guy for real?*

The Duke followed me into the apparatus room, bedroom, kitchen, and was on my heels when I darted into the restroom right up until I slammed the bathroom door and locked it. I stood in front of the mirror.

With the captain on vacation and the lieutenant filling in for him by riding up on the truck, the Duke was now in charge of the engine. I, of course, was assigned to the engine for the entire shift. That meant I was under the Duke's complete command. He had me where he wanted me, and he seemed satisfied everything was going his way.

The Duke was the most imposing man I had ever met, and he had welcomed me with too tight of a hug and an inappropriate wet kiss to my ear. His breath lingered a second too long. I was shocked to smell alcohol so early in the shift. I pulled away. Pulling away only caused his grip to get tighter. His arms ran up and down the length of my body. I bowed up and resisted him. Once I broke free of his arms, I dashed around to stand behind some of the other firefighters while biting my lower lip. At the ripe age of twenty years old, I felt vulnerable and was determined to keep my distance.

When I came out of the bathroom the second time, the Duke was hunched over quietly talking to another firefighter. It looked like more planning, but then he saw me and straightened up while tugging up on his belt, sending me an I-am-going-to-have-you-girl smile on his leathery face.

His plan was now in action with others enrolled in helping, or so he thought. I avoided his grip again and went into the apparatus room. Through the window I saw the Duke talk to the lieutenant. Within a few moments, I was paged over the intercom to come inside.

The lieutenant asked me to assist the Duke with whatever he needed done. I forced a smile with a "Yes sir," and I regrettably reported to the Duke, who was waiting for me to obediently enter his throne room.

The Duke patted the seat next to him. Since I was his project for the day, I was being excused from housework around the station.

*He is being overly nice while keeping me from working which will make the other firefighters angry.*

I needed to show I was not afraid of work, but more importantly, I needed to show that I could get along too.

*Impossible!*

Although I was uncomfortable with everything that had transpired so far, I decided to let the Duke think what he wanted for the time being.

In the early afternoon, we had a small fire. When we returned to the station, I needed to shower. The Duke watched me intently as I gathered my things. I felt his eyes piercing my backside. Young and uncomfortable with all this attention, I prayed I would escape but somehow knew I was wrong. Once the other firefighters finished showering, I walked toward the bathroom. The Duke met me at the bathroom door smiling and promised to protect me from the others.

*Why would I need protection from the others? Nothing like putting the fox in charge of the hen house.*

He graciously opened the bathroom door. "Go on in little lady."

*Little lady? I am six feet tall and can look him in the eye.*

To make things a little more challenging, there was no lock on the bathroom door. So, I stepped in the shower, stripped behind the shower curtain and immediately heard the door creak open.

*Impossible! So obvious—an idiot!*

I yelled at the top of my lungs, "GET OUT!"

I screamed loud enough that there was no doubt the others in the station heard me. The door thudded shut. That was the fastest shower I have ever taken, and I missed some soot behind my left ear. I toweled off and dressed before stepping out of the shower. I caught a glimpse of the Duke looking at my reflection in the mirror.

He frowned and then winked, "Just making sure you're okay." His effort was wasted. I was already dressed. Warmth flared in my cheeks. I reminded myself that this was just a test. However, I was not sure if this day was a test of my determination to keep the job or stop a man who was unstoppable.

*Both!*

I stared into the mirror again.

*You are going to need to be as slick as he is, but you can do it!*

The Duke was perfectly comfortable acting like a teenager around me. If I walked by, he would reach out and grab at my hand. He tried to pull me into his lap.

*This must be how he picks women up in the bar!*

When we sat down to watch the news, the Duke grabbed my chair while I was sitting in it and pulled me closer to him. Just like a teenage boy, he gradually put his arm around me. Each time I pulled away.

During one of the Duke's sniffing sessions, he noticed the soot behind my ear and offered to clean it for me with his tongue.

I let out an "Eeeeeuuuuuu!" I stomped away, furious with his behavior. Some of the firefighters laughed at him, and he gave them all a go-to-hell look. He needed to double his efforts. I was not some liquored-up broad in the bar looking for an easy good time. I was tired of being so close to someone so revolting.

*I should not have to put up with this at work! This is harassment via whack-a-mole.*

That evening, the Duke motioned for me to follow him. I cringed, but did as instructed. He took me by the hand. I pulled away. He smiled and politely grabbed my hand back, showed me to a room and opened a door. "This is where you need to make your bed," he said.

There were only two beds in the room. I pointed to the second bed and asked who slept there.

He smiled. "That is my bed, and you're sleeping in the captain's bed since he's off on vacation."

"I cannot sleep in a captain's bed, I'm just a rookie," I said while biting my lip.

"You will sleep here with me. That is an order," he demanded, in a smoky voice.

*This golden-tongued man thinks he can get me alone in the bedroom? I wanted the protection of the lieutenant and all the Bubbas in the big bedroom on the other side of the station!*

My tongue suddenly felt thick, and I felt I was destined for a challenging battle of wits. I had to end this game with a checkmate. Sure, I was a chess player, but I was not any good. I thought about volunteering to stand the watch all night so I would not have to be in the bedroom with him by myself. Standing the watch would mean I would still be by myself at the front of the station, yet he would still have access to me without others around.

Forcing myself to think, I nervously checked my gear, got something to drink, and watched more TV in an attempt to delay my next move. My thoughts raced, and I was determined to come up with some other plan.

*This is impossible! You are not the victim type. You will fight this guy if you have to.*

Soon the Duke approached me in the watch room. Sliding his arm around my waist he said, "Let's head to bed, dear."

Unraveling his arm, I dropped it and said, "I am really uncomfortable with your behavior!"

"Rookies do as they are told," he reminded me sharply.

Then as if realizing a need to soften his approach, he began to defend his actions.

"You know, I am trustworthy. When I go to bars and some of the women get drunk, I'm the one to step up and protect them. I keep the other men from taking advantage of them." He spoke with a smoky voice. He moved in close and whispered with his breath on my ear, "Relax, girl."

*Relax? What does that mean!*

The Duke assured me he had daughters of his own and would look out for me like he did his own girls. The Duke over-explained things to me, and I felt my blood pressure rise and my muscle tense. The Duke's eyes warned me of even more. There was wanting in those eyes that I did not have a lot of experience with. When he pulled me into his lap, I felt a rising need to scream. I promptly, stood up, growled at him and pulled away. Repeatedly, I hid in the only place with a lock—the restroom. Before I was just worried about avoiding him, but now I was determined to see him fail.

*I would rather have a root canal than to sleep alone in that bedroom with him!*

The Duke reeked of a worldliness that I had never been exposed to, and the more he pursued me, the stronger I felt a rising need to fight. When I pushed him out of my personal space, he just laughed and tugged me toward him even more. The lieutenant was conveniently absent or disinterested in the Duke's behavior.

*It must be a test. I am tested by a slobbering dog—that bites!*

Earlier in the afternoon I was able to escape the Duke's clutches and talk with another firefighter. He mentioned the obvious pursuit by the Duke. I listened and nodded silently allowing him space to talk. He told me there was a bet going down over my sleeping arrangements. "He is planning . . ."

Mid-sentence this firefighter acted a bit nervous and froze. The Duke had entered the room and was watching us. I bristled at his presence.

*He's possessive too. I am not allowed to be friends with anybody else?*

Although I was barely twenty years old, my mind was made up. I was going to make a stand, but I was clueless as to how. I did not want an altercation with him, but I was prepared to slap, kick, and slam my way away from him if need be. The conversation with the firefighter proved the impossible was on the horizon.

That evening, after a couple of runs, I headed to my car to get my bedroll. I barely made it out the door when I realized the Duke followed me into the dark parking lot. He slid up next to me and put his arm around my waist. He pulled me close. I jerked away and almost tripped over him. I was not going to be possessed by anybody and certainly not while on duty. He told me to settle down, "You are safe with me, girl!"

*Yeah right! He really does think of himself as God's gift to women.*

I was way past wishing the chief had succeeded in swinging me back to his station, and I certainly was not looking for a date with a man whose belly hung over his belt buckle. It was suspected the reports on the Duke's "progress" were being broadcast to the entire department, but I had no way of confirming such a thing.

If the Duke succeeded in his quest to conquer me, there would be a payoff involved. I was determined not to be anybody's payoff. Maneuvering for position and protection was never a problem for me at Station 3. I had more firefighter family at Station 3 than any one girl would ever need. They seemed to love me like a sister and protect me. Today was different.

"There are three kinds of men. The one's that learn by readin'. The few who learn by observation. The rest of them have to pee on the electric fence for themselves."

—Will Rodgers

The Duke was about to pee the fence, and I felt something dreadful was going to happen.

The Duke took my bedroll out of my arms and assured me he was a gentleman. He carried my belongings into the bedroom I was to share with him. He placed my bedroll on the captain's bed, turned and said with a wink, "You need me to get you something to drink, dear?"

He tried to be very convincing and authoritative as he leaned against the doorframe and crossed his arms.

*Unbelievable! He really thinks I am stupid?*

I picked up my things and headed for the door.

The Duke slapped the doorframe blocking my passage with his huge arm. "Put those back! You will sleep here," he ordered.

*My, my. He can be ugly when women don't obey!*

He spoke with the authority of a chief, but he made the mistake of dangling his tongue at me in a sexually provocative way. My head was reeling. I was no longer the forlorn little waif walking in the door. My anger and blood pressure rose. My shoulders tensed and jaw clenched. With the mounting discomfort and exhaustion from his pursuit, I knew I had to hold on to my faith.

Something immediately welled up inside me, and I got my second wind. I looked him straight in the eye and said "NO," with more confidence than I really felt.

Like a basketball player on the court, I twisted, ducked and maneuvered under the Duke's arms and darted for the big bedroom. He grabbed at me and tried to stop me, but I was too fast, too mad, and too resolute.

*Whoosh, two points!*

Never before had I feared sleeping next to men, but I had never met an older, mature, powerfully determined, outlaw either.

The Duke punished me by ignoring me the rest of the shift.

*That was much easier than I thought it would be. Check mate!*

There is nothing uglier than a man who usually gets his way and then does not. He acted like I had cheated on him and stolen his money.

*Imagine that? He lost his bet.*

The lieutenant sat up in his bed when I entered the big bedroom with my bedroll tucked under my arm. He said, "Good for you. You did not let him win."

*The test was over. Miracle!*

The Duke did not serve me coffee the following morning. The backroom conversations stopped. I packed my bedroll and gear and carried it to my car by myself. I saw the Duke get in his big Cadillac and squeal his tires when leaving the parking lot.

*Good! I'm glad he is mad. I did not need that kind of friend in the first place!*

When I returned to Station 3, my captain shook my hand. "I hear you handled yourself well at Station 19."

*Oh geez! What does he know?*

A valuable lesson was learned that day. When the inner voice says something is wrong with a situation, take another close look. Nobody has to be a victim. I thought I was going to have to fight him off, instead I communicated firmly, stood my ground, and I grew stronger.

My miracle was sleeping with the snoring Bubbas in the big bedroom where I have always felt safe.

Many years later, after the Duke retired, I saw him on the television. He had been arrested for molesting his daughters.

Dedication: This story is dedicated to anyone who has suffered abuse at the hand of another. Your emergency service workers care when you are hurt. Tell us!

## Gut it up, Girl

My second time to swing was to a station on the north side of town. I did not know these firefighters, but swinging to a different station was cool in that I got to learn new things and meet great new people except for the Duke.

When reporting in at the watch room, I was assigned the coveted position—riding the right side of the fire engine. In the Dallas Fire Department this meant you were in charge of the hose line and putting out the fire. The other team members played supportive roles such as getting water, stretching hose, chopping a hole in the roof, or setting fans for ventilation.

Excitement shot through me once I knew my assignment. Nothing left to do but drag my bunker gear to the fire engine and begin my ceremony of preparation.

Entering the apparatus room, I paused to study the equipment. I made mental notes of where the ladder stuck out from the engine so I would not hit my head when running to the apparatus in an emergency. I also looked for the wet spot from the leaky engine; I did not want to slip and fall. I inhaled deeply clearing my mind and smelled the familiar odor of diesel. I placed my boots, coat, and helmet—weighing close to fifty pounds—on the concrete floor.

I would be positioned in the jump seat behind the officer. I studied the seat a moment and got my bearings. I began the ceremony.

The ceremony always started with my boots. They pointed toward the engine, so if need be, I could hang onto the engine for balance. This was before bunker pants were required to protect our legs and butts. My coat hung on a hook just inside the jump seat. I turned my helmet upside down and checked to make sure I had my firefighting skullcap. This was before we had hoods that protected our face, ears and hair. The old skull cap was to protect my hair but it did a better job of padding the surface of the older helmets. Satisfied that all was in order, I pulled the helmet strap loose and laid it on the belly of the engine. I checked my pockets for pliers, screwdrivers, doorknob strap, rope, gas and sprinkler plugs. All these items might be needed in an emergency, and the extra weight was worth the trouble.

I placed my gloves back in the pockets of my coat in such a fashion that I would know which was left and right; I would not want to waste time sliding them on.

Then it was time for my lifeline—my mask.

Reaching for my mask, I ran my hands over the fittings and then turned it over and checked its gauge. No less than 3000 PSI. I ran my hand over the coupling connection and tightened it hand tight, ¾ turn, just like the rulebook says. I placed it on my face while turning the valve open. I inhaled a breath. I turned open the purge valve and air rushed into my face. A purge valve was good when you were short of breath from exertion. The cool air rushed to your face, and you could suck all the air you wanted. I strapped the mask on my face and made sure it fit, then loosened and checked the straps. It fit over my head easily and tightened securely.

*Check, check, and check.*

Everything was laid out perfectly so if needed, it could all be donned in the dark.

I paused quietly, praying for protection for another shift.

*Thanks in advance, God!*

Performing this ceremony was done with extreme detail just as we were taught at the academy. I handled everything the same as always. I was ready for whatever came my way or so I thought.

It was not unusual to have every move I made studied by others. That was part of being the first female on the job—fish bowl duty. People were summing you up, watching what you did, grading you and drawing conclusions when they were not jumping to them—just like watching fish in a bowl. I was taken aback by all the attention, but at this station I enjoyed not having a bucket of water dumped over my head and my nice clean uniform or being tied to a tree just for fun. This group of men seemed really nice.

Around ten o'clock the bell hit. "Engine 42, Engine 11, Truck 35, Battalion 7, house fire," ordered the dispatcher. Adrenaline shot through my body.

We ran toward the fire engine. I ducked the ladder at the appropriate point and hurdled the water puddle. I tugged on my boots. My right arm went in my coat, then the left. I buckled the coat straps and slung the mask on my back while stepping up and taking a seat on the engine. I donned my helmet and put on my left glove.

The ride was short. We pulled up in front of the small frame house. A bright red and yellow fire showed in the left rear of the small, one-story house. The smell was distinctly different than most house fires. It was not a wood smell, but rather a plastic chemical odor—you could taste in the air.

I pulled a hose line off the engine, stretched it out in a looped pattern and waited for water. I knelt in front of the door and slid my helmet back far enough to strap on the face piece. I donned the mask and made a last minute adjustment to my helmet. I pulled my helmet back up and once it was secured, slid on my right glove. I always held off on the right glove so I could have better tactile feel while turning valves on my self-contained breathing apparatus.

The hose line filled with water and snaked around my legs. The nozzle let out a hiss of air and the hose bulged.

*Show time!*

This fire was going to be a piece of cake, or so I thought. I sucked in the first breath from my mask and headed into the darkened house. My officer was at my side when I was kneeling at the door, but when I stepped inside a few feet and angled to my left toward the fire, I was alone. Smoke had banked down within a few inches of the floor and visibility was at zero, so I supposed he was shrouded in smoke, but near.

I kept moving toward the fire when, suddenly, I was tackled from behind. We fell to the floor in a pile, me at the bottom. I struggled to get to my knees, but there was someone across my back. I thought for a second I was being held down.

*Odd.*

It was usually pretty humorous when this happened—and it happened often, especially in dark rooms and around unseen hose lines, but today was different. It seemed forced, unusual, and awkward. We should have been in tandem, working together, not against each other. We are trained to pick ourselves up and move on, so I did.

As we untangled from each other I heard *shhhhhhhhh*. Air rushed out of the base of my tank at the hose coupling connection. I was losing air! I sucked in hard.

*I cannot breathe!*

I sucked hard again. It was my last breath. I quickly reached to tighten the connection only to have it fall into my gloved hand.

*I could not get any air!*

I sucked on the dry mask, and it created a vacuum on my face.

*No! I did the ceremony. Just like I was taught at the academy! I know the connection was tight! This is impossible!*

Realizing I was bankrupt of air, I ripped the mask from my face. I took in a huge gasp of black, syrupy smoke and began to choke and cough. I detected the chemical odor again, and the smoke was unusually thick. It was time to get out. I broke the cardinal rule and handed the nozzle off in defeat. And *he* was waiting for it!

*He knew, but which he was it? The officer?*

A second and third gulp of thick syrupy smoke and I ran for the door. Outside, I fell to my knees gagging and coughing up strings of mucous filled with thick black soot. My eyes blurred, and sorrow and shame-filled tears worked overtime to wash away the smoke from my eyes. I lay in a heap of defeat, beaten by gang of unruly Bubbas—the Bubba Club.

The driver-engineer at the engine pump panel walked over. I looked up expecting help but heard cursing. My lungs hurt, my chest hurt, my eyes hurt, so why not my ears too?

I hacked, coughed and spit black and all with a stench of failure. I could not speak. It took several seconds before my eyes obeyed my command to open, but when I did, it was all a blur.

There was nothing to say. I needed an ambulance. I could not believe it! I did not want to believe it! We were supposed to take care of each other.

Someone did not want women in the department so they risked my life? No way had I seen this coming.

*Impossible!*

These men started off polite. They were nice to my face, but behind my back they sabotaged my mask. The warm-hearted consideration shown this morning was all pretend.

I willed my body to rise, but it would not cooperate.

Too sick to say or do anything, I could not think. My mind was a mangled mess, and I could not help them or myself. From a disconnected place in the back of my mind rose the question—*sabotage?*

Suddenly, I was saddened, realizing . . .

*Nothing mattered now. They did not need me, and they did not care that I was hurting.*

Once the fire was out, the firefighters changed out masks and rolled hose, but I continued to cough, spit and sputter on my knees. My chest felt like it would explode.

I saw one firefighter throw his helmet toward the engine and yell, cursing me. Other firefighters walked past me as if I deserved to be sick and tortured.

There was more yelling—and then I heard, "I told you so!"

*I told you so? What did they tell me?*

I held back sobs. I held back the hurt, but the suspicion ran wild in my mind. I sensed the truth in the crimson river pounding through my veins and tasted it in the choking black muck I had drawn into my lungs.

"Women cannot take care of this business! Women do not belong," I heard one firefighter say hatefully.

*This sounds like Butch talking.*

Raising my head, I barely began to focus. The men stood over me, looking down with their eyes blazing. It was not one of them, it was *all* of them.

*Double, triple impossible!*

Dropping my head, I cried inside. I had no energy to fight. My chest felt like it was going to burst open and ooze black, gooey pain.

The clock of my beating heart ticked at a faster than normal pace. The odds were stacked against me, and this was a two-faced time bomb. I had to be strong, and I could not give in to panic. I needed an ambulance, but it was clear one had not been called. Nor would the call be made.

"Gut it up, girl," said one cocky firefighter.

*Gut it up! What do I need to gut up? What did I do? What does that mean—gut it up?*

They saw me cry. I no longer cared. I wanted them to see me cry. I wanted them to know what they had done. This was an impossible situation.

When the Capt. said to load up, I lifted my lame duck body and crawled up on the engine.

Riding back to the station, I relived my ceremony over and over in my mind.

*What had I done? What did I forget? Where did I go wrong? Who jacked with my mask! Why did not I pay more attention?*

There was not a shadow of doubt in my mind that everything was in perfect working order that morning. Whoever did this would have to have loosened the connection while still at the station, knowing it would come loose easily once I was wrestled to the ground?

Trusting these men caused doubt to slap me in the face. Left raw, I would never trust again. No longer would I be the social butterfly and pal around with the guys. Moving forward I would keep to myself. Forgiveness left my heart and soul. My certainty of purpose now had a crack in its shell.

Back at the station, the men hit the shower laughing and talking as if nothing had happened. I waited, coughing and snorting black muck. I hovered in the apparatus room not wanting to face the enemy—heartbroken. My mind raced in many different directions. Where they trying to kill me? They were kind to my face, but delivered the ultimate in brotHERhood betrayal. What were they thinking? Somewhere, somehow, somebody's heart is breaking inside for having participated in this level of agitation.

*Deathly agitation!*

Once the bathroom was empty, I entered. My chest hurt and my eyes were so watery I could not see my own reflection in the mirror. It was a bad dream. I sat down removing my socks and tried not to cry, but I could not stop. I was weak and sick and needed medical attention, but I was on my own.

*God, I am alone, but I am alive. How do I muster enough faith for this?*

After a while, I stepped in the shower and let the hot steam loosen the muck from my lungs. Weak, I slid down inside the shower, curled into a ball and sobbed for what seemed like hours. I only wanted a job and was chasing my dream. I wanted to save lives—not lose mine.

Most of the people in the department were fun-loving agitators, but this was not agitation. This was something different. This was sabotage.

*It was threatening! It was real! It was wrong!*

My noisy coughing kept everyone up in the bedroom. Resentment poured forth, and I was asked to leave. I got up and left my nice warm bed for a wooden bench in the kitchen. I coughed and coughed throughout the night when I wasn't crying. It was deep, from the pit of my lungs, gut, and heart-and-soul cough. My chest felt like it was going to explode.

Wondering if any of the men felt guilty, not a single person approached me. No one asked how I was, or if I needed help—no one cared.

*Is anyone ashamed of what happened?*

What would Capt. say if I told him what had happened? He had been so proud that I hadn't delivered him a bunch of bad news after swinging to 19s. He had heard what had happened with the Duke, but I did not tell. I did not want to bring problems.

Thinking about filing a complaint, I realized it was me against all of them. If I made accusations of sabotage, I would never be able to walk in another fire station. Being a scared rookie and not wanting to make things harder on myself, fear roared throughout my body, but I kept my mouth shut until I could think this through.

This was a cold-hearted, no-win situation and would only serve to make me look weaker than I already felt. If anybody told this story, it would have to be one of them. Not me—I would not give them the satisfaction of me whining. I buried it deep inside myself. I was devastated and a multitude of thoughts ran through my mind. Ugly, hateful thoughts ran wild. Darkness consumed my spirit as my faith on fire had been blown nearly out. I could only tell God. It was a lonesome time. It was a challenging time. It was a time of reflection.

*Oh God! What am I supposed to do now? I am hated only for wanting a job. This is an ugly, lonely, and fearful way to live.*

Not only had I been sabotaged, I was dating a Dallas firefighter at the time. When I got off shift, I drove straight to his house, to tell him what had happened and seek advice on how to overcome this situation—he was with another woman.

*Double whammy!*

My heart weighed a ton inside my chest, as it was filled with profound sorrow. Something inside me wanted to give up, quit, walk out, scream, yell, defend and die. I was stopped in my tracks.

> "Be not a slave of your own past. Plunge into the subline seas, dive deep and swim far, so you shall come back with self-respect, with new power, with an advanced experience that shall explain and overlook the old."
>
> —Ralph Waldo Emerson

It was not the first time and it would not be the last time I would face fires like this. Broken, I went home to heal—alone.

*"Face the fire and see the miracle"* came to me in a whisper.

It was as if someone stuck a match and lit me ablaze. The light suddenly burned brightly. I remember reading something that said when your faith is tested, your endurance has a chance to grow. Something sudden and powerful *struck* me. It was the desire to fight—to gut it up, just like they said. What was intended to hurt me, gave rise to a bigger me. Little did I realize, God promises to make something good out of the storms that bring devastation to your life.

*I can gut it up!*

Those impossible words, "gut it up, girl," were suddenly transformed into something useful.

Feeling like a flower with all the petals picked off one-by-one, this attempt would sear my lungs, but would not deter my course. Failure was not an option.

*Gut it up, girl! You will show them and gut it up all right!*

This battle had been won, but war was declared in my heart. It was a war in which I found the miracle inside of the impossible. My miracle came in the form of a determination, grit and stick-to-it that has lasted thirty-five plus years. My faith had now been tried by fire, but not blown out. After two weeks out with pneumonia from black muck, I returned to work—changed. I became more cautious. Those that were overly friendly became suspect. My trust had been removed, and I doubted the genuineness of others.

> "And we know that in all things God works for the good of those who love him, who have been called according to his purpose."
> —Romans 8:28, NIV

Volunteering to ride the ambulance for others became a way to keep from swinging to other stations. The guys at Station 3 loved it, but my Capt. wondered why?

Dedication: This story is dedicated to anyone who has suffered harassment and bullying at work. Be strong, push past the pain and clearly communicate.

## Light Overcomes Dark

Truck 3 had a new rookie today.

*Not me, thank God!*

Somebody else makes the coffee, answers all the phones, answers the main line, greets all the visitors, and does the laundry.

*Yeah!*

Today, I rode the truck, old square wheels, meaning it did not roll on the volume of calls that the engine and ambulance did. It was a welcomed a day off the busy box or engine that chased the box regularly.

Over the radio in the watch room at Station 3, we heard Engine 4 and 18 both report out with smoke showing in a large building in downtown. I got excited. They transmitted two alarms and we were next up to roll.

"Let's roll em, let's roll em, two-alarm fire at Griffin and Pacific.

*Oh yeah, baby! This is going to be the big one!*

We firefighters want to see fire. We were ready to dance with the devil. Our sympathetic nervous systems had already fired at warp speed. Our pulses raced to get blood up to our brains, our heads cleared, and the fight in us kicked in. We arrived at the fire and the smoke had all but cleared.

*Dang it!*

You would have thought we showed up for a funeral. Our heartbeats were raised, and our stress hormones released cortisol—all for nothing.

We entered the *Dallas Times Herald* newspaper printing press room. A light haze of smoke greeted us. The basketball court-sized room looked sterile and freshly painted. It held all the machines that put out the daily paper. Through the smoke, you could see a maze of catwalks and ladders that hovered above the presses.

Capt. had me and the new rookie set up fans to help ventilate the haze out of the building. Then we worked our way and over the ladders and catwalks to a huge press where the fire started. We were buried up inside the building having climbed over a half-dozen ladders and almost as many catwalks. I wished I had stripped down from my heavy bunker gear and mask. I grumbled when climbing the last set of ladders toward the source of the smoke.

*Impossible!*

One firefighter hanging from a catwalk pointed, "Come here rookies and look at this! This is where the fire started."

We shuffled over to get a better look at the fire then suddenly we heard a loud whoosh. The room went dark. There was another whoosh and the building started filling with smoke. We had no lights with us and Capt. and the rookie did not have their masks. My mask, thankfully, was still hanging on my back.

*Miracle!*

Slapping on my face piece, I reached back, turned the knob and took a deep cleansing breath of air. Capt., the new rookie and I started climbing back at a faster pace than our arrival. After climbing down a few ladders, I held the face piece of my mask out to the rookie and he took a long cleansing breath. I held it out to Capt., but he did not take it. He was iron-manning it with that macho-man way of being.

*Impossible!*

We crawled down a ladder and there was another whoosh. The smoke thickened. I was a now worried for the rookie and Capt., but they were moving toward the doors faster because they did not have air.

*Double impossible!*

It is rather lonely in darkness even when others are around. You always feel alone in the midst of smoke, heat and far-reaching darkness. It is just you and the sound of your heart beating, and the air moves through your mask with a Darth Vader quality, "cooo cuhn, cooo cuhn." You have to feel your way up and down ladders, around corners and taking cautious steps into blackness, not a pinprick of light anywhere. Each step into darkness tests your faith and courage. You learn to live through darkness because on the other side of darkness is light.

I heard the Capt. tell the rookie, "Stay calm and come this way." His words were muffled with heavy coughing. It was dark and the catwalks and ladders were disorienting.

Continuing, I maneuver over catwalks and shimmy down ladders. A couple of times I backed up frustrated and went a different way after hitting a wall of ladders that headed up not down.

*Triple impossible!*

The darkest time of the day is just before dawn. It is in the dark moment, in the most difficult and impossible situations, that miracles happen.

Capt. was talking to the rookie up ahead in the distance. Then realizing I was not with them he yelled out to me, "Sherrie, where are you?" His voice gave me direction, and I walked toward it in pure darkness.

*Miracle!*

"Coming," I huffed, while crawling down the last ladder to the ground floor.

No matter how dark life can become, there is always light up ahead. Light overtakes darkness and wins. Light manages to shine through. The darkness was my impossible, and the light my miracle today.

About the time I made it to the exit door, the lights came back on and the smoke began to clear. Outside I found Capt. and the rookie bending over, coughing their left lungs up—saving the right lung for the next fire. We all looked at each other and smiled, laughing nervously.

Looking at them, I suddenly realized how important they were to me not as men, but as friends and family. We all had shared a threat and now shared in a brief moment of joy. Moments like this unite people. Overcoming the impossible through teamwork is an amazing experience.

Today, I felt I was a valuable part of the team. I was thankful for the pinprick of light that shown brightly from the hearts of others, including my Capt.'s heartwarming voice in the darkness. Light, I would eventually learn, would re-ignite my *faith on fire*.

## So You Call This Sleeping

"So where do you sleep," the media asked.

"In a bed," was my response.

That was not good enough. They wanted to see. They wanted to get out a measuring stick and check the precise distance between myself and any other firefighter. Questions were fired in such a manner; you would have thought I was guilty of spooning men at the fire station.

Back in the day, Station 3 had the most private sleeping quarters a station could have at that time. Each bed was separated by a row of lockers but across the aisle was another bed, which was not separated by anything. I was assigned to sleep on the emptier side of the bedroom.

Never has someone sleeping around me bothered me. There are the few exceptions—the Duke and the ones snoring so loud they could rattle the blinds and awaken the dead. This is when I tried to fall asleep first.

There is an array of snores, whistles, and apneic sounds made by the Bubbas after dark.

When riding the box, we paramedics would sneak into a dark bedroom where the engine or truck crew was already sawing logs, and it was difficult to sleep. Begrudgingly, I would pick up my mattress at some stations and drag it into another room. No matter how tired or exhausted I was, once the music started, I could not sleep.

When doing my paramedic internship at fire Station 11, there was one big bedroom before a recent remodel. After cleaning up the station, I went to put my bunkers and bedroll away. I walked in the bedroom and all the beds had been pushed together side-by-side, making one big bed in the center of the room. Hog (nickname for an especially joyful Bubba friend) was lying in the big middle of the beds smiling like a Cheshire cat.

"What's this," I asked.

"It is *our bed*," Hog answered.

"*Our bed*? What do you mean by *our bed*," I asked, smiling back. *Impossible!*

"Well, this is the way we do it around here. We all sleep in one big bed together," Hog said grinning ear-to-ear and letting out a chuckle.

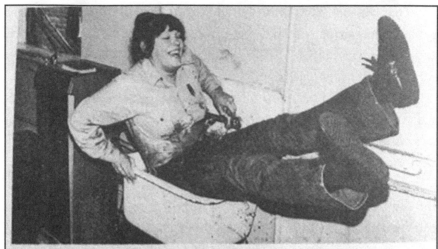

FIRST FEMALE GETS INITIATED! Sherrie Clark, 703(B), has become the DFD's first female paramedic following a six-week internship at No. 11 station. It is a B-shift tradition at 11's to "baptize" anyone who is assigned to ride the MICU.

Sherrie in the mop sink as agitation

We pulled the beds apart. I headed to bed alone, but got side tracked when asked to come and check out something that was really a visit to the mop sink. I was manhandled into the sink used to wash apparatus room floors by several firefighters. The water was turned on and I headed to bed with wet pants. I slipped my pants off and hung them over a chair next to my bed to dry. A problem surfaced as soon as the bell hit. My pants were missing. I sighed. Suddenly, I had visitors waiting to see me get up. I sat in my bed covered up awaiting my pants.

"You're gonna miss a run," said one guy.

I shrugged. "I am not getting up till you give me my pants," I said flatly while frowning.

"Capt. is not going be happy if you miss your first night run," I was told by one of my paramedic preceptor trainers. I flinched knowing he was right.

We heard the captain's bedroom door creak open. Capt. had not heard our ambulance start. We had ninety seconds to roll and our conversation lasted most of it. Everyone in the room scattered and my pants sailed across the room toward me. I got up, slid them on and went down the pole before Capt. could catch me stalling. Never, ever, ever did I make that mistake again as I slept with my pants on or shorts when bunking out.

*Miracle!*

After working at Station 24 down off Hatcher Street, we returned from a fire. Once the guys cleared from the bathroom, I showered peacefully only to have someone knock on the door once I was drying my hair. He wanted to know if I needed anything. It reminded me of the Duke.

While the guys showered, I made my bed.

When I came out of the bathroom the station was quiet and dark. I figured that is just the way they do it here—go to bed early. Even the watchman had turned off the television and the watch room was dark. There was nothing to do but go to bed well before the ten o'clock news.

Never having worked at this station, I was not sure what to expect, so I just made my way to the dark and quiet bedroom, found my bed and hoped for a quiet night.

There was somewhat of a disturbance when the Velcro holding my bunker pants together crackled open. I slid my bunkers down, and suddenly seven flashlights flickered on. Fortunately for me I was wearing shorts—always did after that night of disappearing pants at Station 11.

Laughter was heard through the dark, the lights came on and we stayed up half the night, telling jokes and talking. They just wanted to get to know the female firefighter, and I guess I wanted to get to know them too. I suppose I could have given a negative meaning to some of the things that happened to me, but there was plenty more negative to come, so I picked my battles and laughed at most of the pranks.

Station 35 was one of the oldest and ugliest stations in the Dallas Fire Department. The bedroom was one big room with beds lined around the room head-to-foot. In the center of the bedroom was a pool table.

I slept with my feet at the head of another firefighter who had a severe case of sleep apnea. He could sleep soundly one minute and then go into a coughing, spitting, choking fit the next. His fits were always preceded with a deep-tongued snore. I quickly learned it was better to wake him than let him go off into a round of choking and apnea, but I got tired of having to get up out of the bed because every minute of sleep was precious when riding the box. Plus, my bedroom mate always gave me a good cussing for waking him, so I became extremely creative in saving him from his pending apneic death.

*Impossible to sleep!*

It became a normal thing for me to go to bed hugging a pool stick. Whenever Bubba would start the apneic snoring, I slid the pool stick down between my arms and legs, out the foot of my bed, which was the head of his bed. I would rattle the stick between the headboard rails and then slide it back up into the bed with me where it was hidden by my covers.

Bubba would snort, cough, cuss and then fall back asleep without me feeling personally attacked. Bubba never found out that I was sleeping with a pool stick.

*Miracle!*

## Sam, My Charming

After about four years on the department, I was getting lonely, and all I did was work. My identical twin sister, Gerrie, beat me down the aisle by five years. I guess my mother was worried that I would end up an old maid and told me she was praying for a husband for me.

*Impossible! I was really wanting to investigate until I found my Prince Charming.*

Being a little intense at times, I really needed a hot, steamy, earth-shattering and mind-blowing man, but I could not tell my mother that, so I prayed her prayers would match my passion.

Having dated a few firefighters and police officers, I found out real quick from Ferrelli that I did not want a man from inside our department, or the City of Dallas for that matter. One date with a firefighter, and Ferrelli told me way more than I wanted to know—I now wanted privacy.

*Privacy—an impossible situation at a fire station or in a fire department.*

My next door neighbor told me about a man from the Flint Hills of Kansas who was building a water tower in a nearby suburb. He was the cousin of her co-worker. He wanted a tall girl from Texas, and standing six foot tall myself, I fit his description of the ideal date. Sam stood six feet, five inches, and I did not mind the thought of a tall-drink-of-water myself. I agreed to a blind date.

When I opened the door to my apartment, my eyes locked on his baby blue-greys, my heart skipped a beat, and I held my breath.

*Oh Lord! This I like. This I can handle!*

Once we met, it was clear that neither of us could control what was happening. We fell in love and something beautiful was created. My eyes became fireflies as I had met the most handsome man of my life. This kind of love only happens once.

He was tall, built like an inverted triangle, huge hands and a smile that would melt butter. It took several seconds before I could breathe normally again. Needless to say, the attraction was immediate and mutual. Sam was quiet and mysterious, fun loving, easy to be with and a little shy. During our Saturday night date, we had dinner and danced. When he brought me home it was hard to let him go—he was perfect.

The next morning, I got up, cleaned my apartment and picked up a couple of steaks. Knowing Sam was shy, I called his cousin.

"This is Sherrie, where is Sam?" I asked politely.

"He is standing right here," his cousin responded. Then there was a pause.

"Hello." I could see Sam smile through the phone.

"Dinner is at six." I was smiling on my end of the phone too. It was as if we had talked a thousand times before.

"Okay, I will see you then," Sam responded.

Six o'clock did not come fast enough for me, but when it did, we both knew we were right for each other.

When Sam's company had completed the water tower up in Plano, Texas, their next move was out of the country—to Saudi Arabia.

*They don't appreciate women like me over there.*

Sam came home one night and told me, "I quit my job today."

"Why?" I said hesitantly.

"I'm not leaving you," he said without an ounce of shyness.

*I now had my privacy and my miracle. Mom's prayers certainly matched up with my passion! Double miracle!*

Sam and Sherrie

Thirty-five years of marriage to this man has been the best decision I have ever made. We have shared joy, pain, love and heartache. Every minute with my charming—good or bad, happy or sad—has been filled with memories seared into my mind that make my life complete as does having had someone to love, to fight with, and hot, steamy, earth-shattering, mind-blowing make-up sessions too—miracle!

> "But Ruth replied, 'Don't ask me to leave you and turn back. Wherever you go, I will go; wherever you live, I will live. Your people will be my people, and your God will be my God.'"
>
> —Ruth 1:16, NLT

## Goals

It wasn't long, and Sam and I found ourselves pregnant with our first child. We sat down and added up the cost of diapers, formula and day care. We both had good jobs, but they left us just over broke. I decided I needed to start a business, and I knew how to train others in CPR and first aid. So, I started this little CPR business on the side. I went to some courses to help me learn how to do business and deal with customers. While at the training, I noticed a sheet that the course instructor had passed out about herself. When reading her biography, I was amazed. I was so inspired by her credentials that I took the paper home, whited-out her name and credentials and wrote in my own goals and dreams. The paper flowed well, and it was written as if it were already complete. When reading the sheet I had written about myself, it felt inauthentic, and I remember waving my hand and thinking it would never happen. I posted it on the bulletin board in my home office, and soon it was covered with more important papers.

Several years later when Sam and I moved from our first starter home into a beautiful home in Dallas on the creek, I began to take down those more important papers and found that what I had written had come true. Setting my goals changed my life in a way I never knew it would. I created the possibility of having a huge training company and those dreams came true too. While holding down my job at the Dallas Fire Department, I built a state-of-the-art training and service company which has roughly five hundred instructors in thirty-two states, Emergency Management Resources, LLC.[1] We provided hospital-based as well as business and industry training covering OSHA health and safety as well as emergency cardiac care. We also sell and service AEDs and have added several other products. I have rewritten those goals, which includes writing this book, many times over, and I have always met them.

Our children grew up in a home with both parents working, and I worked two jobs. They survived their childhood and became hard workers, of whom we're very proud. Johnathan and Grant each have provided us with beautiful daughter-in-loves. Sam and I also share one perfect Russian daughter, Anya, and an awesome nephew-in-love. To add to that, we have a slew of precious grandbabies.

From left to right: Johnathan, Sherrie, and Grant, 2007

Anya, my Dorchka (Russian daughter)

*Thank you God for all the double and triple miracles in my family life!*

[1] www.emresources.net

In my private life I faced impossible situations too. My business has had its ups and downs. We all do at one time or another but, because of what I learned from firefighters about joy and being bold in the face of disappointment with a *faith on fire* attitude, I witnessed many miracles too. Sam, my charming, is the best miracle of all. We stay together through thick and thin, no matter what.

## Praying Atheist

We responded to the home of an elderly couple. She was sick—he was mad.

She said to her worried husband, "Honey just pray, God will provide for me."

He responded, "No! I do not believe in your God! If He were really God, He would heal you! I do not want to hear about your God anymore! That is final!"

She nodded her head and smiled lovingly, "Okay, but He really is God."

The old man let out an expletive and told her to stop. He was obviously ashamed of this conversation in front of us.

*Impossible!*

The home they shared was a graceful old home on Swiss Avenue, just east of downtown Dallas. You could tell he loved her. He had given her everything. He just did not love her God.

We loaded her in the ambulance and the heart problem seemed to be getting worse, affecting her breathing this time.

One month later, and "unconscious person" call to the same Swiss Ave address. When we arrived the engine crew was already on scene doing CPR. The husband stood watching, worried. He rung his hands together and shook his head in defiance.

My partner slipped a tube into the lady's throat. I pushed cardiac drugs through her veins. The engine crew pumped her chest. The event was working like a well-oiled machine.

Then, a loud wail, "Oh God! If you're there, help me! Save Mary! Show me, God. Prove to me you are real God. Save Mary!"

*Let something bad happen and people howl to God, like a wolf in a full moon. At least the atheist and I have something in common—I do this too.*

He dropped to his knees and folded his hands—the perfect example of a child kneeling to pray and beg his new God. The white-haired man had huge tears dropping from ocean blue eyes.

We looked curiously at him, then at one another, shrugged our shoulders, but kept pumping, pushing and working. We were working the science side of the equation. The old man was left to do the praying.

*He obviously had not talked to God in a while, so I figured he needed to do his part.*

We got ready to move his wife to the box, and the old man began to calm down, seeming to make peace with God.

The flat rhythm on the EKG screen got more and more squiggly. It went from flat line to ventricular fibrillation. Per our protocol back then, we popped her with three stacked shocks, checked a pulse and started CPR again. After about thirty seconds, Mary opened her eyes for a split second. Then they peacefully closed.

The old man had finished praying and had been closely watching.

"Did you see that? She opened her eyes!" he said excitedly.

My own heart skipped a beat hoping for a miracle.

"Yes sir, I saw that." I said cautiously.

The squiggly line turned back to flat, and we had to keep doing CPR.

"Did you see that?" he yelped again. He began to pace. "Is she going to make it?"

"Sir, I do not know, but keep on praying." I lifted his wife onto the stretcher. The old man kept talking under his breath to his God. On the way to the ambulance, the old man acted feverishly about seeing his wife open her eyes.

We put the praying man in the front seat of the ambulance, and he kept turning to look through the portal to check on his wife's status.

"Did she open her eyes again?" he asked.

"Not yet—keep praying," I yelled toward the front of the box.

I figured I needed to pray too, so that would make a pair of us talking to God.

*Come on God. Give us a miracle. We need a miracle God.*

Once we maxed out all our first line drugs, BioTel, our medical director ordered bretylium–an antiarrhythmic agent. I administered the drug.

*We need a miracle, God!*

We got the woman inside of Baylor Medical Center Emergency. The nurse hauled the old man off to the family room. We transferred the female from our stretcher to the hospital gurney. Before I took her off my EKG machine, I looked at the screen and the squiggly line started coming back. The medical staff took over, and I got pushed aside. We stood around hoping for some miracle. Nothing happened.

*Impossible!*

After a few minutes of watching the medical staff work the code, I gave up and walked away with my head down. There was paperwork to do and a box to clean. Then, I went to wash my hands. Standing in front of the mirror in the bathroom, I talked to God.

*God, are you there? I think the man needs a little help. You have got do something God, please?*

Before heading back to clean the box, we walked by the woman's room and glanced in to make sure we had not left any equipment.

The halogen light in the emergency room cast down from the ceiling. It was suddenly very bright in that room. The old lady was sitting up and talking softly to the doctor. The old man was brought in crying and thanking God aloud for saving his wife. They both held each other tightly while wiping crocodile sized tears from their eyes. It looked like a dream. I was really witnessing a miracle.

He hugged his wife while saying, "I believe, honey, I believe."

"Yes, I know. I knew all the time," she said with a smile.

*Wow! Thank you God!*

*What a miracle! I believe too. I really believe!*

## Madame Pussycat

The door opened and the female inside hesitated, huffed and rolled her eyes, "I wanted you to come to the rear of the house," she said sharply.

"Ma'am, do you have an emergency inside," I said authoritatively.

Hesitantly, she opened the door wide and we entered the darkened home. I could feel my pupils dilating in order to focus in the dark. Dark heavy drapes covered the windows disallowing any outside light.

The Madame controlled everything, including the faint light. A red colored scarf was laid over the lamp, cutting down on its incandescent glory. There were no clocks or any devices to keep one on schedule. Schedules were not allowed inside her home and work place.

The Madame moved like a cat, her hips swaying in a delicate strut. Her voice was a milky purr and she rubbed up against or touched every man in the room and there were lots of them.

Just between the wall and me, I dubbed her Madame Pussycat in my mind. There were at least four or five patrons waiting in the front room. *What the heck is this?*

Madame Pussycat was most definitely in charge, and she moved with a knowing way about herself and her patrons. She smiled, winked and nodded with her hand raised delicately in the air. The men in the room smiled back and obeyed patiently awaiting their turn.

Naive, I was unsure what this place was, but I knew there was something sinister here. My partner whispered "Hanky-panky," in my ear. I felt awkward and very much out of place, but I had a job to do. I looked at the faces of the men sitting around the room and wondered which one was my patient.

Madame Pussycat held up her arm directing us toward the back room. We followed her non-verbal order. She slowly pulled back the drapes and like little children awaiting permission, we entered once she held up her pointer finger and motioned. I felt hoodwinked by her slyness.

Her fluid movements and gentle commands mesmerized the men in the room. I watched them watch her. They were smitten. I felt drawn watching her tantalizing drama until I saw someone quickly duck from one room to another. It looked like an Asian child wearing a slinky, risqué nightie. I shook my head in confusion.

*Impossible! Did I really just see that?*

Two steps inside the room and I saw a man in a semi-sitting position, his pants down around his ankles. Even in the darkness we could tell he was stone cold dead. Madame acted like nothing was happening and hoped to keep us calm. We went from zero-to-sixty in the two seconds it took for us to realize life had left him. That was exactly what Madame Pussycat did not want—someone else in command. This action inflamed her.

We drug the dead man off onto the floor in one quick swoop. The engine crew showed up just in time to start pumping his chest. Lights were turned on and clients started leaving, even though Madame Pussycat protested and sharpened her tone ordering her patrons to sit back down.

We intubated, hung an IV, pushed drugs and defibrillated the man right there in that back room. Activity was at a maximum and not at all the way Madame Pussycat wanted the event to go. She was hoping we would sneak in and out the back door, not disturbing her business for the day.

There is no way to be subtle during an emergency. It is throw down time—time for ACTION! The stretcher was brought in and the patient loaded up. We left the once dark, calm home with the curtains open, allowing in bright light. It is funny how the light changes the way things look, making things clear and precise and sometimes more ugly than they were in the dark.

The front room was now empty of patrons. Madame Pussycat sat staring into space, floored by her own lack of command presence.

Once we got the patient in the back of the box, Madame Pussycat suddenly appeared outside shading her eyes with her hand. The light was just too bright for her liking. She looked much older in the sunshine. Wrinkles formed around her lips and eyes that I had not seen inside the darkened abode. Her makeup was much heavier than originally observed, her long dark brown hair proved to be a wig. The wig had slipped a little to the right looking awkward. I noticed the grey and white hairs that appeared from underneath around her ears.

"Please do not tell his wife where you picked him up," she said. It was a question and a demand all worked into one sentence.

I looked at her and shook my head not wanting to be the bearer of bad news, but most of what we do was subject to open records, except a patient's private medical records. I was busy fighting for life and kept working, ignoring her request. Madame Pussycat realized she had lost another battle and walked away with her head down in defeat.

We transported to Baylor Medical Center emergency room and handed off the full-blown CPR patient to the staff. It did not look good, and the patient was completely unresponsive to any action we took.

When heading out to clean up the box, I saw a pretty, fiftyish female dash from her car into the ER. She had tears of panic streaming down her face. A buddy must have called the wife and told her about her husband. I had guessed this friend was one of the men in the home of Madame Pussycat waiting his turn. When he saw us take the guy out the door doing CPR—well, you know what happened.

We watched the wife run to enter the emergency room, like rushing would make a difference. Unfortunately, it did not. It was not long, and I heard a loud yelp and then a wail from inside the emergency room. Doctors pronounced our patient dead quickly, because no one was doing CPR when we arrived.

People do not realize how important it is to do CPR before emergency services arrives. The American Heart Association, Emergency Cardiac Science Guidelines now proves one of the most important and critical steps to success in reversing death is immediate, high-quality compressions—CPR.

We left the hospital and headed back to the scene and stayed out of service so we would not get another run. I was thinking about the child I had seen ducking from one room to the next. Plus, we had left our blood pressure cuff, realizing it was missing when cleaning up our equipment. I now had two excuses to go back.

On arrival back at the scene, police had now swarmed the place. One officer had already picked up the blood pressure cuff and handed it to us when we pulled up. The police proceeded to ask us what we had found on our arrival. We reported the numerous clients in the front room and the dead man in the back room. I reported the young female with a child's face who ducked from one room to another.

"She looked like a child, but was wearing a nightie," I added.

The police had found illegal drugs, but returned inside on a more intense search.

"We've have had this place under surveillance for some time now," one young police officer shared.

"We knew she was dealing drugs, but we had no idea she was dabbling in human trafficking," said another.

Madame Pussycat was now out of business and in the bright daylight she looked atrocious. She was no longer the in-control, calm man-magnet she had been earlier. Her make-up was smeared with tears, and she looked as if the world underneath her had crumbled. Madame Pussycat's life did crumble when the police brought out three young Asian women found hiding in a false wall inside the house.

*Miracle!*

The sunlight and events of the day sobered up Madame Pussycat, and the police handcuffed her while reading her Miranda rights.

*Double miracle!*

We had to get back in service, and we immediately caught another run. As we took off, I looked back and saw the young Asian women crying and hugging one another. It was sad someone died, but in the face of this impossible situation for the man's wife and family, there was a miracle for three young women. They would no longer be held against their will and forced to act as servants to Madame Pussycat and others.

*It was a triple miracle day for those girls.*

Dedication: This story is dedicated to anyone who has suffered human trafficking.

# Chapter 5

# CLEAR BURNING PHASE

Definition: High temperatures and complete combustion accompany clear burning.

## Your Day to Take a Beating

We entered the jail on the men's side. The bars slammed behind us and locked with an electronic thud. We rolled our stretcher past the first cell. The old man inside rattled his tongue at me like a snake and then opened his trench coat. He had nothing on underneath. I rolled my eyes and kept walking.

*Impossible!*

We entered and loaded our patient on the stretcher. He had beat up his wife the night before. The police ignored his complaint that his wife had got a few licks in on him. Until the bruises turned a dark purple and were painful to touch, then to be safe, we were called to take the assailant to the county hospital for x-rays.

Once in the back of the box, a police officer said, "We will meet you at Parkland Memorial Hospital." He slammed the back doors shut and tapped the back of the box, releasing us.

We headed through downtown and entered Stemmons Freeway headed north. It was 4:45 in the afternoon, which put us in bumper-to-bumper traffic. The traffic was horrible, and we stopped in the middle of Stemmons Freeway at Oak Lawn. Only a few more exits to go, and we would be at Parkland Memorial Hospital. My un-cuffed patient unexpectedly sat up and looked directly into my eyes. I froze, wondering what he was doing and mentally prepared myself in case he attacked.

"I want out," he said flatly.

I yelled up front to Ferrelli, "He's wanting out of the box!"

"Stop him," Ferrelli yelled back.

My patient looked back at me again, and he said in a more determined voice, "I want out!"

I said, "Okay by me, be careful, the highway is full of cars."

He opened the back door to the ambulance and jumped. We pulled up at Parkland Memorial Hospital and went in and told the police what had happened. Ferrelli said, "You should have tried and stopped him."

*Impossible! How could I have stopped him without getting beat up?*

The police officer looked up surprised, "No, she did the right thing. That is all we need is one of you paramedics getting hurt." The officer signed our paperwork, and we cleared from Parkland Memorial Hospital.

"Thank you for thinking I could hold my own with him," I winked at Ferrelli.

"There is not a doubt in my mind that you could have taken him if necessary," he laughed back teasingly.

*Miracle! Ferrelli believes in me!*

Although I matched the guy in stature and weight, he was a woman beater, and I did not particularly feel like taking a beating today.

*Not any day.*

The bell hit and we headed into the Cedar Springs area of town on an aggravated assault call not far from Parkland Memorial Hospital. Two men were still fighting when we arrived. We watched the fight from the front seat of the ambulance.

I looked at Ferrell and said impishly, "Hey, why don't you get out there and stop that fight."

"You heard the police officer, the right thing is to wait," he said matter-of-factly.

*Right!*

One guy went down to the ground and did not get up. Police showed up and handcuffed the second guy. We worked our way over to our patient, loaded him in the box and headed back to Parkland Memorial Hospital. I was in the back of the box with the patient again. He lay with his eyes closed for the first few minutes of the ride and then woke up swinging. I hustled him back on the stretcher taking several punches in the arm, chest and face. With my knee in his chest, I held him down, but his arms and legs flailed like crazy. I was now taking a beating.

*Impossible! Why do people want to go and hate on each other like this?*

Ferrelli pulled into the dock at Parkland Memorial Hospital, slung open the doors and went to work on the guy that had been working on me. Together we managed to get him under control as Ferrelli sat down on the patient's chest; I got the plastic restraints out and tied him up.

Once in the hospital, the triage nurse had us off-load the patient onto a gurney up front. I cut the restraints, and the swinging resumed. Ferrelli got the guy in a headlock, and he started turning blue.

Head nurse Doris, walked up and told Ferrelli to let go, and he immediately let go. You did not argue with Doris. Even the intern doctors obeyed Doris. She was a force to be reckoned with, and she ran a tight ship.

Doris talked to the man like he was a teenager. "Get yourself up on the gurney, and do not move, or I will get my goon to take care of you!"

*Amazing! How did she do that?*

Unbeknownst to us, Doris's assistant had arrived. The patient looked up at Doris and said, "Yes Ma'am," in a respectful and calm voice.

*Impossible! He was nothing but trouble for us!*

Ferrelli and I looked at each other in amazement. This guy had been nothing but trouble and now Doris brought compliance with mere words—then we saw her assistant. He was seven feet tall with the whitest teeth and darkest skin I have ever seen. The assistant's feet were spread apart at the hips and his huge arms hung down nearly to his knees. He was built with his shoulders much wider than his hips. His hands were huge and looked like swollen clamps. He smiled. My head tilted all the way back when I looked up at this man. I felt like an ant.

*Monster of a man! Now that's a partner.*

Doris waved at us to go.

*Yes ma'am.*

I walked away looking back over my shoulder. Doris quickly assessed the patient, and our unruly patient followed every command like a child.

Doris's assistant winked at me as we walked away.

"Geez! Now that is the partner I want on days when I have to take a beating," I said to Ferrelli

*Miracle!*

## Dark as Midnight under a Skillet

It appeared that the Dallas Knife and Gun Club were at it again. The last patient we transported was stabbed in the back which nicked his lung, and he ended up needing CPR. He died.

CPRs always take a lot longer than other runs, especially when they bleed out all over the back of the box. After off-loading this patient at the hospital, we headed out to our glorious job of clean up and decontaminating the box. It seems we smeared blood more than we actually cleaned. We finally broke out a bottle of peroxide, poured it on top of everything, and watched it bubble. Peroxide works miracles on blood. It cleans blood out of clothes, off skin, off backboards, floors and ceilings of the ambulance.

Once the box was clean, we took our aching backs to BioTel, the radio room for North Texas paramedic services located inside Parkland Memorial Hospital. BioTel is where we talk with the doctor and get orders for treatment and drugs while in the field. We washed up, grabbed a drink and sat stretching out our tight backs. My back ached like crazy—always did after a CPR—it was hard to stand up straight.

*My aching back—Geez!*

Within a few minutes of sitting down, the phone rang. It was fire dispatch. The city was out of ambulances, and it was time to hit the road.

*Impossible, never-ending shift!*

We inhaled deeply; exhausted from all the activity today as we were approaching eighteen runs for the day, and the sun had only been down a few hours. We left Parkland Memorial Hospital and headed back toward downtown via Stemmons Freeway.

The radio blared, "703 shooting. Patient out front of apartments."

My partner slapped his hand against his leg frustrated with the endless day and lack of food. We gutted it up and soon pulled into the apartments in South Dallas. Our flashing lights cast weird reflections off the apartments. It looked eerie.

*Boogey man is in there!*

Ever get that spooked feeling? The kind where to you start to pray, even though you do not know what you are praying about? Suddenly it was so dark outside, you could cut it with a knife.

The complex was known for gang activity, but tonight it was in total blackout. There were no porch lights, no lights on inside the apartments. No signs of anything, but it smelled of trouble. Something was not right about this place tonight. It was as dark as midnight under a skillet.

We pulled our penlights out and squeezed the triggers to see where we were stepping and immediately found droplets of blood but no patient. We followed the blood up the stairs.

*Impossible! What happened to "patient out front"?*

Most of these apartments were boarded up, but we knew our way around, because we had been here too many times. Firefighters, unlike police, do not do anything quietly. We stomped up the stairs and my partner stifled a laugh as I tried to steady my nervous shaking hand. We kept following the blood droplets right up until we saw the glow of a cigarette at the end of a long hallway.

*Is that my patient?*

The cigarette lit up as someone inhaled deeply on the end of it. I stopped mid stride and yelled out, "Fire department. Is anybody hurt?"

The cigarette was tossed aside, and we heard footsteps in the distance. We walked toward where we saw the cigarette butt, but the smoker was gone. We both turned toward one another as if seeking out some kind of strength.

*Hmm . . . Was that the shooter or the patient?*

Cautiously, we backed up to where we last saw blood and began following the droplets again. The droplets made a sharp left at a little alcove, and I saw blood smeared on a knob of an apartment door in the shape of a question mark.

Approaching cautiously, I knocked loudly shouting, "Fire department!" The door creaked open, and I repeated my identity a second time, speaking into twilight.

*Nothing, but silence and darkness—impossible situation!*

Looking for my partner's eyes for strength, I could not see them. I wanted to know if Bubba was experiencing the same level of fear as I. I figured that since he was a man, he would not say so.

I whispered, "You want to back out and wait for police?"

Suddenly, a wooden plank on the other side of the apartment complex creaked. We both froze mid-sentence not wanting to be a target. Freezing in place made us the perfect target. I held my breath and looked for an exit sign. Not finding any exit strategy, I thought about the importance of finding a restroom, because I was about to pee my pants.

Unexpectedly, a moan came from inside the bloodied door. The moan was enough for me to perk-up and forget about myself and run toward the voice in need. I followed the blood and the sound into the gloomy void.

*God, help me!*

I saw movement in the dark back two rooms.

*Oh no!*

"F-E-A-R has two meanings: Forget everything and run or face everything and rise. The choice is yours."

—Zig Ziglar

Choosing to rise, all I could see was darkness, but by faith, things suddenly became a little brighter. Facing the fear that possessed me, I swallowed hard and refocused my penlight on a three hundred pound black male holding his left hand to his chest and breathing in short, quick breaths. I approached cautiously. Squeezing the trigger on the penlight again, I redirected my tiny light to the cold black steel gun in his right hand. It was a big, heavy, semi-automatic, gun.

*Impossible! I hate guns. What were we thinking entering this place without police?*

My heart stopped for a split second, but I quietly chastised myself for being afraid. I figured if I am going have faith, I might as well show that faith by getting the job done. I gutted it up and grabbed the gun, while trying not to plaster my fingerprints all over it. Tossed it into a dark corner, and we went to work on our patient.

*I touched that gun! I don't want my fingerprints being on any gun!*

My patient's eyes were fearful, and I am sure I reflected back the same, but I kept moving like there was two hundred miles of faith up ahead.

My patient's raspy breathing became faster than normal. I looked concerned and told him, "Hang on man, we are going to take care of you."

The blue and white Dallas Cowboy jersey my patient was wearing was now soaked in blood. I whipped out my paramedic shears and began to cut the bloodied mess off to expose his chest and bullet wound. The bullet entered the chest one inch above the left nipple.

*Geez! This is not good. I hope it didn't nick his heart! It has for sure got his lung.*

The wound spit blood out every time the man coughed or breathed, and it sucked in with a whoosh noise when he inhaled.

*Sucking chest wound.*

I heard the blessed word, "Police," and yelled into the darkness, alerting them of our location.

One officer entered and advised us to, "Stay put until we secure the area!"

My partner and I were busy with our patient, but in the back of our minds we were in no hurry to head out with police in SWAT team mode with their pistols drawn.

We heard a lot of noise and police announcing, "Come out with your hands up."

Before long, police were crawling all over the place. We were no longer alone.

*I always feel better when backed by the brothers in blue.*

Once our hefty patient was loaded into the ambulance, we hung two IVs of Ringer's lactate, trying to replace all the blood he was losing. We put the cellophane from my partner's pack of cigarettes on the man's sucking chest wound. We taped it down on three sides and left the forth side open to relieve pressure. Every labored breath caused the cellophane to suck in. Every time the patient breathed out, a little blood bubbled to the surface, but for the most part it had slowed the bleeding. The cellophane or Vaseline covered 4 x 4 was all we had back then, but it worked.

Before we could take off for the hospital, our patient's breathing became short, his belly quivered and then his eyes rolled backward.

*Impossible! Not another CPR!*

He sucked in one last breath, and then his pulse was gone.

The fight was on. Back-to-back CPRs was not a good way to start the night. We had the stretcher sitting up hoping to help his breathing. I dropped it back flat, and my partner began pumping his chest. Every pump brought more blood to the surface.

Double *impossible!*

It is hard to fight a bullet that ricocheted inside somebody's chest, but we threw caution to the wind and gave it everything we had and then some.

*God help us!*

This was when I prayed—in the heat of the battle. I prayed a lot on the box. Sometimes it was "God, help me, help him," or "God forgive him, whichever way this ends up." Other times it was just a, "God help me and my aching back."

Kneeling at the patient's head, I set up the laryngoscope and endotracheal tube. Peering into my patient's now pink frothy throat from all the blood mixed with air, I looked for the triangular shaped vocal cords. Seeing them, I slid the tube in and secured it in place with tape. By now, Engine 6 had shown up and helped us set up the CPR machine called the thumper.

*Thank You God, it was my turn to drive.*

Driving meant a brief moment of resting one's back while in route to the hospital. Riding in the back was a gamble to say the least: trying to push drugs and keep the thumper in place while holding on for dear life while hitting every bump, railroad crossing and pothole at warp speed. With a dying patient we took corners on wheels and drove like a bat-out-of-hell.

Wheeling into Parkland Memorial Hospital, I opened the back doors of the box to the thump, thump, thump, thump, thump, whoosh noise of the thumper. The thumper's noisy sound always got people's attention. Not in a good way, just a get the heck out of the way. Our stretcher was covered with a bloody patient and in between his legs was clutter from IV's, drugs, and oxygen that powered the thumper. We bypassed triage and headed directly to trauma room 2, since our first CPR of the night, although now dead, was still in trauma room 1.

We stayed long enough to see the doctor crack the patient's chest open, suck out some blood and manually pump the heart. Witnessing the quick and efficient work of the doctors was always intriguing. Seeing the heart, the blood, the vessels and organs was always viewed with interest and wonder.

"Nope! This one is cooked too," the intern said when finding the hole inside the chest. He stuck his gloved finger through the hole showing us the damage. I did not flinch an inch.

Death officially occurred under the halogen lights of the emergency room. There was just too much damage to his heart and lungs. The bullet had also pierced the pericardial sac around the man's heart. Once the sac filled with blood, it squeezed the man's heart like vice grips and shut it down.

I had looked into the man's eyes inside that dark apartment. They begged for my help, my intervention, and I willingly gave it my all. Now his eyes glazed over and stood fixed in place; he no longer needed me. His eyes did not shut and the huge hand I found gripping tightly to the cold steel black gun had relaxed open for the last time. Then the reality hit me—this is the end.

*I hate guns!*

There was suddenly something sweet and innocent about this man. He was somebody's child, brother, father. He was gone in the blink of an eye. I never understood why my patient needed to die; I closed my own eyes in frustration and increased my level of hate for guns to an all-new level.

*Triple impossible!*

My father was a hunter. Once when cleaning a gun, it went off and the stray bullet whizzed by my twelve-year-old body. The blast shattered the window behind me. It scared the bejeebers out of me, and I got sweaty and sick to my stomach. Tonight was no different.

We headed to clean up the box and then to BioTel to rest—our backs were in spasms.

*My hate for guns is at an all new level.*

In the bathroom I looked in the mirror and was shocked at all the blood splattered around my uniform. There was even a smudge of blood smeared on my cheek. Paramedics had not yet been issued gloves until the early 1980s, and I washed my bloodied hands and watched the blood of this patient circle the drain and out of my site.

*God, why?*

Closing my eyes, I was thankful and safe, protected by God as always. We had unknowingly entered a scene that was very dangerous. We came out alive. It was a miracle for my partner and me.

*Miracle! Thank you God for always keeping me safe.*

## Unbearable

Whoop! Whoop! Whoop! The siren for the most part was ignored by downtown traffic. It was not really anybody's fault because there was no place to go. We drove onto the sidewalk to get around the traffic.

*Unbelievable traffic!*

We pulled up to a man doing jumping jacks in the middle of Main Street. His face contorted with panic. He stood next to a flatbed truck loaded with huge spools of one-inch thick cable. Cable was being run underground in the downtown area, and his job was to drop off the spools at each site.

We hopped out of the box and ran around the side of the truck. At first glance there was a lady on the ground. Well, that is not exactly right. It was half a lady, a huge wooden spool filled with cable and then the other half of the lady. We found out later, it was the man's wife. He screamed at a fever pitch. This screaming made it hard for us to understand what he was saying.

*Impossible!*

"All I had to do was drop this cable off. She tried to help me, back me up." He cried. "Help her . . . God! Help her." He dropped to his knees and wailed uncontrollably.

Dropping to my knees, I checked her pulse and raised my eyes to Ferrelli. I did not even have to say a word—he understood. This injury is "incompatible with life." Nothing to do but cover her body with a sheet. The sheet confirmed what the husband already knew, but he was still in denial.

*Unbearable!*

Denial is an interesting emotional phenomenon. Is it the will not to face problems? Or is it an attempt to protect oneself from reality? Or better yet, is it a way of retaining our sanity when experiencing the unbearable? I have found no reasonable answer.

It was unbearable enough for us, but that did not touch what the husband was going through. After all, how do you tell someone their loved one is dead? The words catch in your throat and you cannot swallow to clear them. There was no training for dealing with death back in the 1970s and 80s. To say, "She is dead," is too quick, much too easy and yet much too complicated. Are you supposed to say something kind, loving and truthful? There is nothing you can say to make something unbearable—bearable.

We said what we needed to say with our eyes cast down toward the ground. No eye contact—less pain for us.

With nothing to do for the woman, I went to her husband. He was a mess. All I knew to do was to hold and hug this complete stranger. He only wanted to close his eyes, turn away and wake up from this terrible dream. Holding on in spite of his resistance, I shared in his agony for a brief moment. His resistance finally ended, and he cried a bucket of tears into my shoulder.

*Push past the pain, Sherrie.*

"Oh God, why?" He cried over and over.

*Yes, God, why?*

His loud sorrow-filled tears became my silent ones. It was unbearable, but this was a part of what rescuers do. We will hold you during your pain.

Sometimes, I get mad at God and demand to know why. How can this be fair, God? How can the unbearable be part of your divine plan? Then I walk around sheepishly hoping I did not make Him mad with my whining and why.

This kind of pain breaks the shell that encloses our character and you learn to trust and lean not to your own understanding.

We must walk through the impossible and the darkness in life. On the other side of darkness is light.

*Impossible shift!*

Dedication: This story is dedicated to emergency medical technicians (EMTs) and paramedics out hitting the pavement every day and facing the negative things in life while serving citizens of the world.

## The Flooding Fire

When the Engine 18 reported out with smoke showing on the tenth floor, we headed that way, determined to back up the brotHERhood. Engine 18 made a quick attack on the fire and seemed to have it under control when we got there.

When we arrived, the incident commander assigned the rookie and me to take sump pumps down into the basement. All the water they were putting on the fire above was draining down through stairwells, electrical raceways and hidden spaces in the walls flooding the basement. Our assignment: pump out all the water from the basement. There was reportedly *important equipment* that needed protection from the water.

Carrying two sump pumps, the newly assigned rookie and I descended the stairs. We would rather be in the middle of fighting fire, but we had our assignment no matter how unflattering.

The water rushed by our feet as we descended into the bowels of the building. When we finally made our way down—the basement was already flooded several feet. I was standing in water up to my knees. I radioed the command post and told them that we had set the pumps, but that it was a losing battle. They were already fully submerged and doing no good.

*Any equipment needing protection from the water was already completely drowned.*

It was still unknown the type of equipment command was concerned about, but that really did not matter at the moment. Doing what needed to be done was the job in front of me, and I was going to fulfill on my assignment.

After standing around in the basement for an hour with water now up to my waist, we were told to pick up the pumps and bring them upstairs.

*We had failed our assignment.*

We could not see the submerged sump pumps and struggled to find them in the deep water.

I was a fairly new senior fire and rescuer officer given my first real responsibility, other than saving lives, and I could not even find the equipment that was assigned to me.

*The "geez" factor was at a premium.*

Finally we stripped off our bunker gear and dove underwater to locate and rescue our equipment.

Soaked and having failed, we ascended into the presence of command and received a butt chewing for drowning our equipment and failing at our assignment. Shortly thereafter, we were told to load up and go home—our help was no longer needed. We never got to see any fire, and that was the worse punishment of all.

*Okay, so it was not a perfect world. I tried hard, did the job as best I could and got a small butt chewing and left without dancing with the red devil. No big deal, right? Not exactly!*

We returned to Station 3 and the captain called my rookie partner and me to the hose rack. If you wanted to *whup-up* on someone, you invited them to the hose rack. Capt. just wanted privacy away from the others.

*What did we do wrong?*

My partner and I showed up at the hose rack, just under the shadow of downtown Dallas and Baylor Medical Center. I was prepared for a level-two butt chewing, although I was not really sure what I could have done differently. Capt. paused, inhaled deeply and proceeded to calmly tell us that while soaking ourselves in the basement water, we were absorbing polychlorinated biphenyls (PCBs). PCBs were widely used fluids in electrical apparatus, which were the transformers located in the basement. Capt. told us PCBs were cancer-causing agents.

Due to PCBs environmental toxicity and classification as a persistent organic pollutant, the United States Congress banned production in 1979.

Quietly, I stood looking at my rookie partner and then back at my captain. Silently I shifted from one foot to the other, as if engaging my mind to understand. It was as if my mind hit a blank wall, and I could not think. I could not process the seriousness of the matter. I stood there thinking of literally nothing. My mind raced to find an angle, an advantage, a reason—nothing came to mind. I sat down next to my captain. I swallowed and jerked my neck to the right trying to pop the sub-luxed vertebrae in my neck back into place, as if would make it all go away. It did not work. Capt. and my partner stayed quiet.

*Impossible!*

As if someone struck a match and lit dried brush, the gravity of the situation flashed in front of me. I rose up and as if wearing some kind of impervious bulletproof vest, I said, "Okay."

*What else could I say? I took a bath in a cancer-causing agent for over an hour. Will this keep me from having children? How long will I live? God, are you hearing this? I need you.*

With youth on my side and a flash of certainty of faith, I got up and headed to my mosquito filled bathroom attached to the apparatus room, which was my only place to have any real privacy at Station 3. I closed my eyes and bowed my head and said, "God, protect me from this stuff, whatever it is."

Firefighters asked me how I felt a few times. Some looked sad for me. I just smiled back. I was literally living with fire licking at the edges of my faith, but my *faith on fire* was lit and burning brightly. I went back to work and never gave it further thought until writing this book. I am still amazed and assured all is well.

*Miracle!*

## Twenty-Year-Olds Do Not Die from Heart Problems

The bell hit. I flipped on the flashers and Ferrelli turned the siren to a loud wail. We made a quick right out of the station and a sharp left onto Gaston and headed into downtown Dallas. After a hard right at Pearl, we pulled up in front of a large multi-storied office building housing an insurance company. The report was an unconscious female on the fifth floor.

Inside we found a twenty-five-year-old female thrashing about on the floor. Her color was good, one minute she seemed to answer questions, and the next minute she flailed. Her behavior did not really make sense. It was not a seizure, it was different, and I could not put my finger on what was happening. There was no doubt her brain was not receiving enough oxygen, but why?

*Hypoxic? Hypovolemia? Toxins?*

Ferrelli and I loaded her on the stretcher and headed toward the box. Before we could make it out the door, the girl went flaccid. The sight of her jolted me into action.

"She's quit breathing," I said to Ferrelli.

"Surely not," he said as he leaned over to pick up some equipment.

"She's not breathing!"

The tone of my voice was all it took, and Ferrell dropped the equipment and focused in on the girl. At twenty-five years old, she still had a full life ahead of her.

We increased our pace from a hustle to a dead run. The elevator was so tiny, we had to break down the stretcher to fit it inside on the way up. Now it meant we had to sit the unconscious patient straight up and fold the stretcher again. The elevator door opened, and it was full of people. We ordered them off and commandeered the elevator. I continued attempting CPR with our patient half sitting, but she was significantly slumped over and the compressions were not effective.

Reaching ground level, we flattened out the stretcher, and I pumped her chest while running alongside the moving stretcher. We both lifted her up inside the box and went to work. Ferrelli had already called for an engine for extra help. I jumped out of the box to get the thumper from an outside compartment, twisted my knee then hobbled back inside the box.

"Twenty-year-olds do not die from heart problems," Ferrelli said.

"What?" I said, distracted by assembling the thumper.

He repeated himself, frustrated at the situation.

"Okay, they usually do not, but this one is dying of something," I retorted.

A police officer opened the back of the box saying," This is the patient's sister. She works in the same office."

The female looked at us nervously, unbelief in her eyes. The thumper was now pumping her sister's chest with a thump, thump, thump, thump, thump, whoosh.

Ferrelli was peering down the patient's throat, threading a tube into her lungs. I was now sticking a needle in her vein; I taped it down and then stabbed her IV port with epinephrine.

Sure it was not a pretty sight, so I pointed to the front of the cab and asked the police officer to place the sister in the passenger seat. The officer started to shut the ambulance door. The sister resisted, opening the door back open with her arm.

She looked up tearfully and said, "She has a hole in her heart. She was born with it."

*Impossible!*

Ferrell and I looked at each other puzzled. This information proved nothing to us at the moment. We were set to fight for this girl's life all the way to the hospital and then some. Ferrelli drove to Parkland Memorial Hospital, and I held on for dear life in the back of the box, while trying to deliver epinephrine every five minutes and sodium bicarbonate every ten.

We arrived at the hospital and rushed passed triage like a fast moving storm rolling in from the west. Our pace was enough to clear the halls.

The thump, thump, thump, thump, thump, whoosh from the thumper caused medical students to trail us like ants at a picnic into trauma room 1. Within a few minutes, they opened the girl up, cracked her chest and began to manually massage her heart. Blood poured out of the girl's chest cavity like she had been shot with a high caliber rifle.

*Double impossible!*

Ferrelli and I looked at each other, realizing our efforts were all for nothing. A second later, the lead intern found the hole in the girl's heart and called it. It was 10:55 am. The time of death was the last thing the nurse noted on the patient form. It was the end of life. For nearly an hour we fought for that life.

*Sometimes it seems we do all we can for nothing!*

Doris, the head nurse at Parkland Memorial Hospital, entered trauma room 1 and ordered all the extra staff people out. The room cleared except for Ferrelli and me. Doris patted us both on the shoulder simultaneously. She knew us and could tell we were worn out and frustrated. Doris could just touch us on the shoulder and it was enough to convey, "Good job," or "I know you're tried." The tiniest acknowledgement at the right time can make a world of difference. That day Doris made a difference to us, as we felt defeated.

*Doris likes us and she cares about paramedics. Her support is a miracle.*

Exhausted, we lugged our own bodies out to the box and started to clean up. This is when our backs ache. Everything tenses when you're fighting for life while hunkered over in the back of a box.

There is an unwritten rule we follow when our patient dies. You go about your cleaning and preparing for the next emergency, but you do so quietly. It's a moment of quiet, of respect in memory of a life. It's an unwritten rule, but most paramedics observe this rule. We do not take life for granted. Our hearts ache momentarily, but we move on. The next call for help is all we need to move on.

This quiet time is spent thinking things like, "How could I have made a difference," or "Why do twenty-year-olds have to die?" Sometimes I just ask God, "Why?"

I have learned it is what it is, even though I may will things to be different.

"I trust in you, LORD; I say, 'You are my God.'"
                                              – Psalm 31:14, ESV

## Shoveling Chicken Ice

Have you ever been to a chicken slaughterhouse? Chickens look a lot different when you see them being plucked and then hung on a hook that roams through a chiller room or on a conveyor belt. Above the chill room was an antiquated fan and ice room. That is where we found him with a shovel at his side.

He spoke Spanglish, but it was easy to see what had happened. The shaved ice was covered in blood. Truth be known, the ice probably saved his life by constricting the blood vessels around the stump, slowing the bleed. While shoveling ice he lost his footing and slipped. The fan had no covers or guards. His foot sailed right into the fan spinning ice around the chilling room below. His foot cut off at the ankle. It was a nice clean cut. He did not even feel it. It was a miracle he did not fall through that fan and down onto the conveyor below. The engine crew below in the chiller room, along with slaughterhouse personnel searched for the amputated foot among the chickens splattered with the man's blood. Through the spinning fan, I watched one person pick up every chicken on the conveyor belt and look under it.

The injured man kissed his Saint Christopher necklace and breathed, "Blessed Mother Mary," in Spanish.

We dressed his stump, taped it into place, and then attempted to put him on the stretcher. He was the independent type and was irritated with himself. He wanted to walk even though he was missing a foot. He cursed his own stupidity under his breath while resisting my moving him.

"Señor, yo ai-yur-di," ("I will help you,") was my weak attempt at communicating with him.

His color took on an ashy appearance, suddenly he went weak, and giving up, he let us lift him over toward the stretcher. I immediately slipped on ice. Not wanting the fan to stop me, I quickly took a knee. My foot stopped just before it hit the spinning fan.

As I went down, the injured man went with me, his dressing came off and his bloodied stump landed in my lap. He started cursing me in Spanish.

*Impossible!*

"I found it!" One of the guys riding Engine 6 hollered up at us. I glanced down and one crewmember who held the foot up in the air for us to see. I looked back at my patient; he was staring at his own foot below.

We lifted the patient again and left the ice room looking like the mound of a strawberry snow cone.

We wrapped the amputated foot in a multi-trauma dressing, bagged it and placed the bag on ice. There was plenty of that around.

*It is a miracle I did not end up like our patient—without a foot. Thanks God!*

## Gang Fight

The bell hit and we headed to East Dallas for a reported stabbing. Swinging into the parking lot, we witnessed about twenty young Latino men fighting. Some wore red and others wore blue. Our lights and sirens scared a few of them off, but the others did not seem to care and knives swung in every direction.

One knife was jabbed toward the belly of a guy wearing a blue bandanna around his head. Another knife seemed to hang high in the air then swing downward into the neck of another guy wearing red. We called for police, code 3, and waited in the safety of our ambulance for backup.

One young man suddenly slapped his bloodied hand on my window. The sanguine fluid smeared downward as he sunk toward the ground. It looked like something out of a horror movie, but we hopped out and helped him inside the back of the box. I lifted him toward the stretcher. He was holding tightly onto his right arm with his left hand. I pried away his hand in order to place a bandage on his bleed. When he let go, blood spurted uncontrollably across the back of the box and then up at the ceiling.

*Arterial bleed.*

I slapped a handful of 4 x 4s onto the pulsating mass and wrapped it tightly as my patient's eyes rolled backward, and his head flopped onto the stretcher—he went unconscious.

*Still breathing.*

Putting oxygen on him, I turned to check in with my partner. He was outside the back of the box and was suddenly rushed by three Latino males. All were bleeding from different places. They talked in Spanish so fast it was hard to understand anything they said. But it was easy to tell what was wrong. We called for two more ambulances.

The police showed and people scrammed. A few individuals kept fighting until police stopped and handcuffed them. A few came and sat in my ambulance holding bloodied bandages on their wounds. I could not leave my unconscious patient, but we were bandaging kids and young adults as fast as we could. Claret body fluid was everywhere in the back of the box. Finally, another box showed up, and we handed off most of the patients except a few minors ones and our unconscious patient. Then we hauled it, code 3, to Parkland Memorial Hospital.

On arrival at Parkland Memorial Hospital, we rolled in a fury toward the trauma hall. Our patient's blood pressure was dropping every minute. After we off loaded our patient and provided a verbal report to the doctor, we headed back to clean up the box.

Another ambulance showed up with six patients, all minor injuries and all wearing red. As we made it out to the loading area, another ambulance showed up with seven patients, all minor injuries, but they were wearing blue.

*Impossible!*

It was not long until the fight was on inside the emergency room.

A dozen squad cars showed up to the emergency room, code 3. They entered with guns drawn. The police had everything under control in short order. But it was definitely a little exciting there for a few tense moments.

*Wow! The excitement and drama was at a level ten.*

A few years later, the hospital installed metal detectors providing limited access to Dallas County's primary hospital emergency room.

# Chapter 6

---

# THERMAL LAYERING

Definition: Thermal layering of gases is the tendency of fire gases to form into layers according to temperature.

## Slithering and Sliding

It was about dusk. The sun had set, but the western sky was still ablaze with remnants of blue light. People began to flip on their headlights and traffic was moving smoothly through the central business district of Dallas.

After a great day on the lake, a young man was pulling a boat through town. Crossing the Trinity River Bridge, he jolted into one of our Texas-sized potholes. The impact caused something from his boat to drag. He stopped and got out of his truck and walked around to the back of the boat to inspect the damage.

The car behind him stopped and flicked on a blinker, planning to change lanes. The traffic coming from behind at sixty miles an hour did not cooperate.

Tires squealed as people slammed on their brakes and metal crunched together in a domino effect, all falling in the boater's direction. When the last domino fell, the car behind him locked his breaks to rcsist lunging forward. Then the rear-ended car rocketed forward toward the boat. With no time to think, the young man standing at the back of his boat jumped off the bridge and into the Trinity River bottoms. To stay put meant he would have been sandwiched between the oncoming cars and his boat.

When we arrived, we pulled up beside the boat only to be told our patient had gone over the side. I peered over the bridge and could see nothing but dark. I hollered down, but could not hear anything in return, except my own echoing voice.

"Are you sure you saw him jump?" I asked one bystander.

"We are coming for you," I promised my patient lying somewhere below in the dark.

We were situated just south of the river and the only way to get to the patient was to hike it over the levy and down into the river bottoms. We pulled the box over to the edge of the bridge, set the fast idle, flipped on some extra lights and headed into the abyss. The only thing missing was the sign that read, "Abandon all hope, ye who enter here."

Leaving the levy, I stepped off into the river bottom and sunk down into mud up to my ankles. Stepping back, my foot came out of my shoe. After retrieving the shoe I tightened my laces; they were stringy and muddy and felt odd in my hands as if trying to tie together two slimy snakes.

Suddenly, I heard some mad howls in the distance. I felt a counter surge of fear.

*God, I am gonna need help in this blind world.*

Forcing some tall grass to lay sideways, I hoped it would prevent me from sinking down too far in this sodden mess. I stepped again, my shoes filled with water. Something moved in the dark up ahead, I jumped back, screamed aloud and froze. My sympathetic nervous system picked up pace and my pounding heart was now throbbing in my head. My spirit sank.

*"Oh God, help me."*

My partner laughed, but not for long.

Standing still, I tried to focus my eyes, but whatever had stirred in the dark slithered away.

Saving lives was fun right up until this moment. I wanted to rip people from the jaws of death, but that ripping did not include heading into a dark level of hell in Dante's Inferno. This was the particular level of hell where things below the surface eat you. Fear slashed out at me like a whip, and I choked back bile rising in my throat.

*Impossible situation!*

We made our way forward only about six feet through the slurry, dragging the backboard and a cervical collar (C-collar). The backboard snagged a few times, and the harder I yanked, the deeper I sunk into the mud. After pulling the backboard free, I placed it out in front of me and crawled up on it and then helped pull my partner free of the dark quicksand.

*A clamor of success—if we only had two backboards we could use them as a board walk.*

If there was anything that was going to bite in the dark, it bolted or went unconscious once I slapped the ground with the board. We stepped up on the backboard, and it sunk down into the muddied grass, but it kept us afloat. Once we made it to the other end of the board, we kicked grass over on its side, stepped off the board, moved the backboard forward again and then stepped back up on it. We leaped-frogged through the slimy river bottom by way of a single backboard.

*Is this some wicked scheme or do I really have a patient down here?*

Straining madly to see in the darkness, I finally heard the words, "Help me. Over here!" The traffic slowly snaking around the wreckage above drowned out his weakened voice.

At this point my partner's right leg sunk into the mud, up to his knee. I negotiated my way over to him and tugged. He was trapped. Our skin was crawling with all kinds of muddied things.

*God, this murky environment appears to allow all to enter, but none to escape! Help me please!*

It was really more of a begging request than a prayer, and each step forward in the soggy river bottom was a step of faith. I realized my rookie partner prayed too. I know because I heard him after all, we were sharing a foot and a half wide board only six feet long.

Our flashlight started to fade. I pulled out my penlight used to check a patient's pupils. Does a penlight shine in total darkness? I hoped it would, but it provided barely a pinprick of light.

*How could things get any more impossible? It was dark as midnight under a skillet but filled with slime!*

Once my partner was free from the mud, we stalled out retrieving his shoe. Once we freed the rebellious shoe, we started making our way toward our patient again. The closer we got to him, the louder the traffic above distorting his weakened voice.

It was that voice in need and my prayers that kept me moving forward in faith.

I slapped the board in front of me, this time hitting something. The board moved sideways, and then the grass around the board moved too. I screeched, my voice hoarse and shrill. Freezing and studying the dark, I could not see a thing. Pointing my penlight to the right, I picked up a pair of orange-yellow eyes peering back at me—they were not our patient's eyes. The black pupils appeared to be diamond shaped. My teeth began to chatter ferociously, and I was bathed in terror at this nightmare path.

I gasped, "Oh God," while staying alert for any more movement.

*Creepy-crawlies mixed with gators!*

"Surely there are some snakes out here," my partner said excitedly.

"That was not a snake, it was big, like a gator." I hesitated and then took another step of faith into the dark, watery world.

*God, I am not sure I can keep going.*

This was early in my career and I was usually riding shotgun with a more experienced paramedic. Tonight, I was leading the team and my plan only included the next few steps into darkness. I wanted to hold my head in horror and cry, but I was determined to succeed against this dreadful swampland and save that voice shrouded in darkness. So, I held my head up, gritted my teeth with determination, threw my shoulders back and marched on into this underworld with my *faith on fire* like I had been trained to do by the men at Station 3.

*There are those that think they can and there are those that think they can't. They are both right! I can do this!*

If we did find our patient, I was not sure we could get him out considering everything we were facing. We could barely move the backboard forward in this chaos. How were we going to move the board with the patient riding it?

We also needed more light. I keyed my now mud-soaked radio, believing in the system we had at the Dallas Fire Department and said, "703 to 660."

"Go ahead 703," the dispatcher responded.

"We are performing a rescue in the Trinity River bottoms and need another engine and truck to set some lights from the bridge. We also need the helicopter on alert-go status." This not only gets a helicopter warmed up, it tells it to take off and head our way.

"Received, 703," the dispatcher responded, confirming my request.

We kept working our way cautiously toward the patient as the truck and engine crew showed up. They set lights from the bridge above pointing downward in a 60 x 60 pattern, the minimum lighting pattern required for the incoming helicopter. The lighting allowed us to pick up the pace as we leap-frogged with the backboard. It took another ten minutes to make our way through the dark chasm.

"Over here! Help me! Over here," said the lost voice.

"We're coming," I pledged in my loudest voice.

Before we reached our patient, I heard him breathing in short, quick, and loud breaths. We found him lying flat on his back in the middle of slimy darkness with all kinds of creatures slithering around him.

He prayed aloud, "Thank you Jesus! Thank you God! Boy! I am in love with both of you. Thank you God."

*It's a miracle our patient is doing so well. Double miracle we made it this far, but now to get out? God, I am going to need a triple miracle tonight.*

Since our mud-covered patient was able to talk and pray aloud, we knew he would be okay. Not much assessment goes on in this kind of environment anyway. Our patient was talking and breathing so we focused on packaging him up for transport. We could not do that fast enough. We slopped around on our knees in the mud hoping nothing would slink upon us.

It was not long and we heard the chopper blades above. The wind under the chopper began to blow hard. The helicopter had to land between the R. L. Thornton Freeway and Corinth Street bridges.

There was not much room and even less light for visibility. The helicopter hovered longer than usual making sure its blades would not hit the bridge.

Finally, after muffled radio contact between the pilot and our dispatch requesting the lights be moved, it hovered low but did not land in the mud. We crawled toward the helicopter on our hands and knees, struggling to drag our patient now strapped down to the backboard. Our arms and legs were already covered in slime, and the chopper blades now slung mud in our faces and hair.

*Like I need this pandemonium to get any worse!*

My eyes burned like coal and so did those of my patient and rookie partner. We had our patient close his eyes. With one eye cracked open, we slopped forward.

To provide continuity of care, one of the medics on the helicopter had to get off and let one of the DFD paramedics ride with our patient to the hospital. This did not set well with the nurse who was ordered to dismount her sparkling clean helicopter and step into my unknown world of muck and slither.

*Oh yeah! I forgot about this rule.*

My rookie paramedic sheepishly asked if he could ride in the helicopter. I only had to think about that for a split second.

"No," I said with confidence. "Your job is to deliver her [the nurse] safely to Methodist Hospital."

We lifted off and hovered above downtown Dallas momentarily. I watched the intern and the persnickety nurse begin their struggle back through the river bottom toward the box. They got smaller and smaller the closer we got to Methodist Hospital located just west of the river. It was a dream that I sat in that perfectly clean helicopter with my patient; both of us covered head-to-toe in slime.

*God help them navigate back safely because I have the backboard with me.*

I feared they were either crawling or sinking.

*Thank you God for getting me out of that nightmare. What a miracle!*

## Tidal Wave of Tears

It felt odd—something was different—something that was not supposed to be.

*Do the body and spirit battle separation?*

Maybe it is that battle of separation I felt. I prayed as I descended into darkness. Death has its own distinct feeling. It is a unique stillness with a decisive end. Death is a quiet statement that lands with a loud thud on the hearts of loved ones.

The call we received was reported as a hanging. Ugly dark thoughts came to mind when we entered the scene. Thoughts of suicide is always one of them—erotic asphyxia another.

Our words were carefully chosen and crafted as we swiftly tiptoed around the devastated parents. "Which way, sir?" we asked gently.

They were bound together in each other's arms. Their hearts ripped out, eyes overflowing with grief filled tears. They shared together and now lost together.

There was nothing one could say, nothing anyone could do except watch as their hearts flow outward with a tidal wave of tears. These are the unrelenting emotions that flood a parent who contemplates burying their own flesh and blood—their child.

*Teenager—boy.*

Entering the scene, thoughts were running wild.

*Who was it? What was their life like? Were they loved? Were they sad? Was it an accident? Was it purposeful? Why?*

We jimmied the door to the teenager's room. It creaked open easily. The room looked innocently youthful. Basketball, smelly shoes, posters of athletes, an unmade bed, and clothing wadded and dropped on the floor—nothing but young adult, yet somehow childlike, belongings.

We moved swiftly through the room as our eyes swung to the closet. We tugged open the closet door. It was unusually heavy and dragged on the carpet. I closed my eyes and held my breath—hoping beyond all hope that it was not what I already knew it to be.

The body hung lifeless, still, ashen and blue. Face white as a sheet, arms and legs unusually blue from blood pooling in his lower extremities. His arms hung loosely at his sides, and his feet and toes pointed down. A chill swept across me and the hair on my neck and arms rose as if saluting.

A quiet scream came forth inside me, but no one else could hear it. The screaming was in my head. I was suddenly without a voice, a will. I stood and looked for an answer.

*Why? Why a child? God, help me understand! Help me put this into perspective. Help me make sense of it all. God! Answer me! Please!*

We moved the door out of the shadows. The face of a child appeared mounted on an adult sized body.

I mumbled an, "Oh my God," or was it, "Oh God, no!" I cannot remember.

Understanding was so far away that I could not grasp it. I could not believe my eyes. I took a deep breath, my hands shaking.

We have to assess the patient. We had to say whether he was dead or not. We had to declare the obvious. So opening a pocketknife, my partner cut the child down, but avoided the knot.

"Cut them down, but we want to study the knot," one medical examiner had told me years ago.

The body's weight fell forward and dropped into my arms. The movement caused the pressure in the lungs to release trapped air, and

I felt the exhaled air on my shoulder. A shiver crossed my body, and I tensed but knew this meant nothing in the grand scheme of things. The blood in this body was no longer pumping—creating a thriving pink. The spirit had long departed. The child was stiff as a board with rigor mortis. I placed the body gently and respectfully on the floor. Dependent lividity says it all—gravity did the final job and pulled all the blood flow to the lower regions of the body turning the feet an unusual blue. This tragic event was incompatible with life.

The mind numbing effects set in—there was nothing else we could do for the patient.

*God help me. It's a child! His life had barely begun.*

Asking the parents for the child's name was on our list of things to do. These parents would cling to the name of their child for the rest of their life. This name, their miracle, their joy now ripped from their hearts.

Shaking my head, I tried wishing it all away. It did not work. This day would mark the beginning of an end; the end of life and a beginning without the child they loved so much. I could separate myself from this, but his parents would never let go.

*Pushing through the pain is what separates the winners from the losers.*

I wanted and needed to do something, this was someone's child for heaven's sake! The parents needed to know that we moved purposefully and did everything within our power to help.

My head was spinning out of control. My prayers unanswered.

*God, why?*

Bargaining silently, I cried at God's lack of response, and then I realized my will did not fit into His plan.

Pausing, I held my breath, kicking in the parasympathetic nervous system, slowing my now throbbing heart. Finally, everything slowed to a sensible level so that my thinking kicked into gear.

Having a job to do did not change the fact that I did not like it. My job was to do it. No more questioning or stalling.

We covered the body out of respect. Covering also prevented staring and studying all the unique features that create wonder.

*Why now? Why him? Why these parents?*

It was time for all the uncomfortable questions. You must ask lots of them. What medications was he on? Was he allergic to any medication? What were his last activities and last meal? Was there any other pertinent medical history? We will not use this information. We only wrote it down for the medical examiner. It helped piece together the impossible story of death.

We stand guard once a death is proclaimed, especially an unexplained or unusual death. We stayed at the scene awaiting police and investigators.

My entire adult lifetime has been spent fighting for life in the face of death.

*God, I have had my fill, more than my fair share of this.*

If you were to look into my eyes, you would see the eyes of a woman who is far too familiar with death. I have witnessed the battle, the separation and the last breath. Enough is enough. No training prepares us for this. Our hearts are torn, but we must go on. Nothing can stop us in creating miracles, even in the gory face of death. There was no victory to be found here.

"Where, O death, is your victory? Where, O death, is your sting?"
—1 Corinthians 15:55, ESV

Dedication: This story is dedicated to all the parents who have lost their children for whatever reason. There are no words.

## Second Driver

When I was young and there was something to be decided, I usually spoke up and had my say—I got this from my mother. I took one for the brotHERhood with the city council, mayor, fire chief, firefighters, and television stations watching.

Management was getting rid of the position of second driver in order to make way for more promotions. I did not really understand all the ramifications, but I thought people should take a test and pass just like I had done.

While sitting in front of the Dallas city council dressed up in my best suit, I simply said, "We need to keep the rank of second driver."

*Piece of cake. No problem! Right?*

A man sitting on the city council stood up pointed his finger at me and said, "You are a racist young lady!" It was Al Lipscomb, the man on television from my youth. This was the man that marched up and down the streets mad about something when I was a child. Now he was mad at me, and I was clueless as to why.

*Impossible! I thought we were both fighting for the same thing?*

Al and I have a lot in common, but I did not see how the word *racist* had anything to do with second drivers inside the fire department.

*Now I am the dunderhead.*

It was shared with me later that the black firefighters wanted to do away with the rank of second driver so that more minorities could make rank quicker. I had no idea this was the reason. Shrugging my shoulders, I studied and made driver-engineer.

*Problem solved! Miracle!*

## Licensure for Paramedics

Another fight brewing in our department was over paramedics. Back in the day when I was a thriving paramedic, firefighters did not really seem to appreciate our work. One particularly old crusty firefighter told me while sucking on a cigarette, "If I drop dead of a heart attack, y'all don't come and pick me up. I would rather die instead."

*I will just save this old buzzard just to prove to him wrong!*

Firefighters did not care about paramedic issues, and they nominated me as the state firefighter's representative to Texas EMS Advisory Council (TEMSAC). This is a position appointed by the governor of Texas, but I do not think firefighters knew that at the time. They just knew it was something regarding the "bambulance" as some lovingly referred to it, and they did not need any more of that.

Once on TEMSAC, I heard there was an assistant chief in Dallas Fire and Rescue who wanted the position. He was too late. They had already nominated a female to do a man's job.

It seemed simple to me. We needed licensure for paramedics.

*Did I tell you they sent a female to do a man's job?*

EMS Article

At the time, I also doubled as the president of the Texas Association of EMTs and served on the board of directors for the National Association of EMTs. Some firefighters thought I was just a token female, filling a very unimportant position. At the time, I was the only local non-Chief EMS person to be included. I lived, ate and breathed EMS work. So I knew what paramedics wanted, and I was determined to get it for them.

I sat with the power of the politically connected firefighters and the state association of EMTs and paramedics behind me.

There was one small problem. The medical community did not want the change we wanted, which was licensure for paramedics. Paramedics wanted to be recognized as a professional group of healthcare providers. There were disagreements over the possibility of paramedics crossing over to become nurses and nurses crossing over to become paramedics. Basically, there was a fear that paramedics would try and set up "doc-in-the-box" shops and cut doctor's offices out of business.

*Impossible!*

It was reported to me that the Texas Medical Association was fighting the bill that we firefighters introduced. Not only would it create licensure for paramedics, hopefully it would do away with the biennial state examination for EMS personnel.

Firefighters can be slow at times, but they are also some of the smartest people I know. They also hire good lobbyists.

At our Texas firefighters association, I met a man in charge of lobbying. I told him what paramedics wanted—we wanted licensure. We exchanged numbers in case there was something firefighters wanted at TEMSAC. It was simple. I asked the brotHERhood of firefighters to introduce and back the EMS bill.

The State of Texas EMS bureau chief, a good friend of mine at the time, predicted failure for the bill and was careful not to be seen as too friendly toward me because the medical community had power in our state. This was the kind of power that held his job in their hands. He all but assured me of failure.

I waved my hand laughing. "This is going be like taking candy from a baby," I said assuredly.

*I was bluffing. I learned it from firefighters. It is part of our faith and expectation and we rarely are disappointed.*

Having had no idea what was about to happen, I did the only thing I knew to do—I asked firefighters to support the bill. The brotHERhood delivered in a mighty way.

In the face of the Texas Medical Association's (TMA) power with the legislature, firefighters smacked them down. The bill passed. Licensure for paramedics became a reality. As an added bonus, EMS-degreed programs began rolling out in our state. The state requirement for biennial testing was changed from a law to a rule, but testing continued.

*We won the big issue—licensing.*

So the granddaughter of a load-and-go mortician of yesteryear, a girl who rode a Cadillac ambulance with only a first aid card in the beginning of her career, a female firefighter because someone said "No you can't," finally made a difference to those she held so dear—the uniformed men and women of the Dallas Fire Department. I also became one of the first licensed paramedics in the State of Texas.

The medical community was so mad about firefighters winning they asked the governor to sunset the TEMSAC committee. TEMSAS went away, and I went away—but licensure for paramedics we got to keep.

*Miracle!*

## Driver-Engineer

It was a slammer of a storm. Droplets flew sideways like knitting needles, thunder snarled, and lightning flashed. We hunkered down inside Station 7, not getting a single run. With all the wood shingled roofs in our district, one little sliver of lightening and we could be fighting fire the rest of the shift.

*I don't wish anything bad, but if someone is going to have an emergency, I want to be the one that puts out the fire or rescues them.*

Eventually, the sun came out and stretched its arms around our little piece of the earth. The air smelled of fresh rain and the streets glistened brightly from their spontaneous cleaning.

We were called out on a structure fire, and I was the new driver-engineer on Engine 7. We were the first apparatus to arrive and reported out with a five story-parking garage. Heavy black smoke poured from the top floor.

We knew it must be a vehicle, but there were rules to transmit two alarms on anything four stories or higher with smoke or fire showing. We followed the rules, transmitted two alarms and then ordered a booster.

Boosters are small trucks with a pump and power takeoff, otherwise known as a PTO. They carry enough water to douse a car fire. Boosters are also high-profile vehicles that can take more difficult terrain. We usually only call them to grass fires or high-rise parking garage fires, because they also fit under the low hanging rafters.

We walked up the stairs of the garage and once on the fifth floor we found a vehicle completely engulfed in flames. Among the flames, you could see a figure of a person. It was too late. Nothing to do but wait until water arrived.

There was no doubt that the person was dead, but it is horrifying to watch someone burn and not be able to rescue them.

The police showed up. They were on the phone with the deceased's wife. The deceased had called his wife in an upset over a fight they had earlier. He told her his plans of suicide and his location. The depressed man detailed his actions to his wife as he struck the match. She heard whoosh and then screaming and the phone went dead.

The booster finally arrived and we put out the fire, cracked open the hood, door and trunk with a pry bar while awaiting the arson investigator. An empty gasoline can was inside the trunk. The vehicle was completely scorched and black.

This tragic event was ruled a suicide.

*How does one stay positive in the face of this, God?*

## Fighting for Women

It appeared that females were not being mentored in the department because all the prized positions went to men. I asked the chief of the department for an open-door meeting. I told him that the command technician and chief aide jobs always went to the men. Women deserved a shot at some of them.

If they wanted women to move up the ranks, they needed to mentor us, to expose us to things and give us a fair opportunity to live out our potential. Simply hiring women was not enough. We wanted locks on bathroom doors. We wanted equipment that fit properly. We wanted some of these prized positions. The chief was actually receptive and listened.

Some of the shorter women faced unique challenges. One female was so short, when she got in to drive the ambulance she had to put a first aid kit behind her back in order to reach the gas pedal. This was due to the new mobile data terminals (MDTs). Shop personnel had pushed the benched seat all the way back and permanently placed the MDT so the seat could not be adjusted. I was clueless with my long set of legs, but I knew this needed to change and the chief agreed.

*Wow! He really seemed to care. Awesome!*

Moving city hall was a slow and arduous process, but our chief was proactive. As ambulances were changed out, the newer ones had bucket seats so the MDT could be placed in the middle and the seats could be adjusted. Slowly locks appeared on bathroom doors. Some stations that did not have bathroom doors got them.

Shortly after my visit with the chief of the department, Chief Baker, deputy chief of area two(the southern sector of Dallas), called me and requested I come in for an interview with him for a command technician position.

*I now have a chance to learn something new!*

Dedication: This story is dedicated to the women inside the brotherHERhood.

# Chapter 7

# HEAT TRANSFER

Definition: Fire communicates and heat is transferred by three methods: conduction, convection, and radiation.

## Driving Deputy Chief

The interview with Chief Baker had gone well. This chief's relaxed manner made it easy for me to talk and be myself. Not long after the interview he called me and told me I was selected for the job. I was shocked!

*Miracle!*

"After ten years working on ambulances, Wilson was assigned to drive a deputy chief. It is a technical and demanding job requiring her to know the whereabouts at all times of every firefighter at a fire and track their positions on a status board. 'You have to know your business,' says one chief, 'and she did it extremely well.'"

—Dallas Observer

Finally I could see what this chief business was all about!

There were two sides to being a command technician. At the station, I performed most of the chief's administrative duties, which included balancing the manpower across the city and time off, along with other assorted jobs, with the exception of discipline. At fires I was in charge of the command post, overseeing radio communications, the tactical work board and tracking personnel at the scene. The command post was responsible for pinpointing the areas firefighters were assigned, so that we would know where to search should a firefighter go down during a collapse, explosion or other disaster.

Each time I reported for duty, I knew I had a bird's nest on the ground. I loved this job! Chief Baker was my favorite chief. I was treated fairly and respected, and I learned more in the few years I worked for him than in my entire career. I learned more about the computer, fire tactics and strategy, decision-making and the organization. The officers under him were pretty amazing as well. This chief and everyone connected to this office had that winning attitude of *faith on fire*, but it was like *faith on fire* on steroids.

*I love it here!*

The deputy chief of area two included the central business district and the southern sectors of the city. I helped manage five battalions, twenty-five fire stations and 249 people. We responded only to major incidents such as two-alarm fires or greater as well as injured firefighters. We spent a lot of time during the day at city hall getting administrative assignments. In the evenings we stayed up late doing five-year response time studies.

## Eighteen-Wheeler Turned Over

Dead Man's Curve is located in the southern section of Dallas. It is where Hawn Freeway ends and feeds into the central business district. An eighteen-wheeler truck driver realized too late that the highway would end. He had seconds to make the choice to negotiate the sharp right turn or plow smack dab into the south Central Bridge. He slammed on his brakes and the semi-trailer loaded with eight thousand gallons of methyl-ethyl bad stuff screeched to a halt. The cab jack-knifed, and the truck tipped up on its side.

"It teetered for a minute," the truck driver said. He scampered out of the cab unhurt but shaken. The flammable product inside the truck poured out and into the Dallas storm sewer. This was not the first of these types of accidents, and it would not be the last until this road gets redesigned.

First-in crews laid a hose line in case of fire and reported they could not plug the leak. By the time we responded in the deputies' vehicle, fumes were permeating the air and evacuation of the neighborhood had begun. Since we were operating in freezing weather, Dallas Area Rapid Transit buses were ordered for temporary shelter for the citizens removed from their homes after midnight.

Deputy Chief Baker and the battalion chief discussed the ramifications of the product in our drainage system. I was instructed to make a call to Streets and Sanitation and get maps of the drainage system—and they wanted the maps delivered, code 3, with lights and sirens. Dump trucks loaded with sand were also ordered.

Within a half hour the maps were delivered, and we laid them out on the hood of the chief's car. The Streets representative pointed to our current location. We followed the map and found where the drainage system became an open basin.

Chief said, "Sherrie, do you know where the cemetery is just east of here?"

I answered in the affirmative. We ran, code 3, to the cemetery. An engine crew met us there, and we broke open the locked gates. We crept through the dark cemetery with flashlights. At the back of the cemetery we found a big drainage ditch. No product was present, meaning we beat the lethal flow to this point. This was the last place to make a stand and prevent the fuel from entering the Trinity River, contaminating water and wildlife.

The truckloads of sand had followed us in, and firefighters started shoveling sand into the ditch fast as they could. Once they finished building a dam with the first layer of sand, the product began backing up. They doubled their efforts dumping sand from every side and it was a race whether the sand or the eight thousand gallons of fuel would fill the basin first. Firefighters, like most times were determined to win, and they did it again.

*Miracle!*

The EPA had been notified. A representative from the EPA called me back on the chief's cell. I told him about the truck, the fuel, the drainage system, and about our plan to head it off at the cemetery—all successful.

*These two chiefs are amazing. I am learning from the very best! It is a miracle just to be offered this kind of opportunity.*

The City of Dallas received an award from the EPA for our quick response to the potential disaster.

*With good team dynamics, you can turn the impossible into a miracle.*

During this event we had clear roles and responsibilities, clear communications, mutual respect, constructive intervention, we knew our limitations, and we shared knowledge and constant re-evaluation of the incident. Most incidents work well when team dynamics are in full play. These are some of the very same team dynamics I teach for the American Heart Association in the Advance Cardiac Life Support and Pediatric Advance Life Support courses.

*I feel so useful, respected, and part of a great team!*

For the first time in my career, I found someone who really invested in me. Chief Baker taught me things I would have never learned at the station. He pushed me harder and further than before on learning the computer and putting out amazing work.

Chief Baker has been a double thrown down (best of the best in firefighter terms)!

*I am blessed to have this man in my life.*


Dedication: This story is dedicated to awesome leadership that touch, move and inspire us to be all we can be.

## My Pretty Little Head Will Roll

Agitation is a regular thing at the fire department. We were told in a paramilitary organization we needed something to lighten the load, so to speak, and agitation was an acceptable way to relax. You cannot work at the Dallas Fire Department without experiencing some form of agitation. Today, it was my turn to dish it out.

For over a month, there was someone with the combination to our shift's refrigerator lock, and they were stealing and eating our cake. Our shift *loved* cake. Every other shift we made a cake, ate about half of it, and locked it in our refrigerator for the next shift. The deputy chief was off on vacation, and a battalion chief was riding up to fill in his place. I whined to the visiting chief about our cake being stolen, again.

He laughed out loud and said, "You are from Station 3, and they are notorious for punishing those who steal food and drink! Do something about it."

I thought back to the orange juice fiasco at Station 3, and my stomach knotted up for a moment, then a devilish smile came over my face.

Thinking about his comment "Do something about it," I decided to make a stand. It was not long I had explained the plan to the Bubbas. These were the older, about ready to retire, "I do not want to get in trouble" Bubbas. I convinced them that I would take any heat. During the day, the chief officer and I made a swing by the local drug store.

Late that afternoon I set about my plan. I had one round cake pan that was new and one that was old and beat up. I mixed the chocolate cake mixture and filled the new pan with half of the batter. I then proceeded to add my melted concoction to the balance of cake mixture. I poured the now doctored cake mixture in the old beat up pan. I warned my guys not to eat any cake in the old beat up pan.

Once the cakes cooled, I iced them both, and I served the good cake for dinner. Once dinner was out of the way, I went about cutting the spiked cake in half, stacking one layer on top of the other and then placed it in the plate of the cake we had already eaten. It looked like half a cake. I covered it up and locked it away in our refrigerator like always.

*My pretty little head is going to roll.*

Once the thieves ate the stolen cake, I heard stories of diarrhea for the entire shift. One person actually reported off sick and went home. I shrugged my shoulders and acted surprised about the incident, but somebody gave me up. No idea who, but his initials started with B.U.B.B.A.

*Impossible, but not a real surprise!*

Once my deputy chief returned from vacation, he sat me down one-on-one, face-to-face, and acted serious. He told me there were reports that I had spiked a cake and members were ill and reported off sick as a result. I sat smiling and smug.

*I could be in real trouble!*

"Chief before we go any further, if anyone is admitting that they got sick from eating a spiked cake, they are also admitting to you that they broke and entered our refrigerator and stole the cake in question. It was not their cake to eat," I smiled, sufficiently pleased with my effort to explain.

Chief took a long swig off his cigarette and released the smoke into the air above his head. He sat quietly thinking. He thumped the butt of the cigarette onto the ground and cracked a crooked smiled while rubbing his forehead with his thumb and little finger.

"Well, I guess that just about does it then. They are not willing to admit to that, so this discussion is over," the chief said while standing up and walking away.

*Chief Baker is an awesome man! He is so generous and kind to me. Whew! I could have got in some real trouble for that.*

Never again did the other shift break and enter our refrigerator. The chief never said another word to me. The double dose of Ex-Lax did the trick! There is only one thing left to say. I was trained well at Station 3.

*It's a miracle that I got away with this agitation. Ha!*

Working for Chief Baker was a win-win, but while I was there, I was writing articles for the *Industrial Fire World* magazine. Regularly, I passed those articles out before being published to the chiefs on all the shifts and requested feedback. When a chief I had worked with in Chief Baker's office was promoted to assistant chief of communications and lost his PIO, he knew I could write, and I was drafted to fill this job. Up until now, the PIO position had been a non-uniformed position.

## Public Information Officer

Dallas City Hall is a cantilevered building that slopes at a 34° angle. The building has a buff-colored concrete and looks as if it is top-heavy. Three cylindrical pillars appear the hold up the structure. Dallas City Hall served as the city hall in the movie RoboCop. I reported to this futuristic building excited by my new challenge.

Dallas City Hall

"The role of the Public Information Officer (PIO) for Dallas Fire-Rescue (DFR) has many facets, not the least of which is making sure that when a significant emergency occurs, he or she provides accurate and timely information to the media, so that the public remains informed about the scope and nature of the situation."

—Dallas Fire Rescue website

As the PIO, I connected with the media. I prepared press releases, wrote brochures, and even coordinated accident demonstrations for high-school students with Mothers against Drunk Driving (MADD).

I loved responding to all the department's major events and getting to see everyone. Every multi-alarm fire was like a fire station family reunion, but my job was to gather information.

The reports from the commanders were important to preparing press releases, but hearing the stories from the Bubbas and clearly understanding their efforts, opened doors for me to acknowledge them.

When riding an apparatus you witnessed single events, but now I was called to every major event where the department was involved. My job was to find out what happened. It was amazing to see the miracles that went down inside a twenty-four-hour shift. Nobody really knew about them. Another tradition we have in the fire department is we do not acknowledge miracles—as miracles. Working to create miracles is just business-as-usual for firefighters. God uses emergency responders this way.

*I am gonna share this!*

If you are not looking for miracles inside your life, you will not see them. I was on the lookout for miracles, and I found plenty of them. I really felt the love of the brotHERhood during this time.

"In the mid-1990s, Wilson was looking for a change. For a year and a half, she served as the department's public information officer where she trained 1500 city workers in the city's new 3-1-1 non-emergency city-service system."

—Dallas Observer

The best of the brotHERhood still loved agitating me. When I showed up at a fire dressed up with a fresh hairdo, I made it a point to steer clear of some of them. A dirty glove smeared on a freshly painted face did not look good on TV. In spite of their orneriness, it was my turn to take care of them and show off the miracles that they were up to.

The following event was one of those miracles. The men and women of the Dallas Fire Department transformed this hell-on-earth event into wonderful stories of rescues and efforts.

## Six-Alarm Motel Fire

In the middle of August 1996, it was a hot and sweaty day. I was headed to bed but the pager went off, and I headed into the South Oak Cliff area of Dallas instead.

A jilted lover had crept on scene at a local motel. He dribbled gasoline out of a can in a breezeway. He really did not want to kill anybody; he only wanted to get his girlfriend's attention. As a macho-man, he would teach her a lesson. He would teach her who was boss.

He fetched the matches out of his pocket, withdrew one and struck it against the sandy paper on the bottom of the matchbook. He lit his cigarette first and threw the match down.

*Poof!*

It was just a little flickering of fire. He turned his back and strutted away far enough to watch the show undetected, waiting in the shadows.

No alarms went off. They had been disabled by the motel manager/ owners, and no bells alerted those sleeping. The motel manager/owner was also a little on the lazy side and had stacked some broken furniture against some of the exit doors. Turning the motel into makeshift apartments created a perfect target for an arsonist.

A few of the people who lived inside the apartments had scrambled to put out the fire, but no one called 911.

With his initial plan thwarted, the young arsonist stomped away in defeat. His anger grew, and he grabbed the gasoline can and headed back to fulfill on his goal. He poured even larger puddles, creating a bigger fire, hoping his lover would be awakened and need him. He struck the match, studied the dancing flames a moment and swaggered off confidently.

Screams went out, and the same resident-cavalry that responded before to put out the fire went into action. This time discussions went on about what they should do.

"Man, we should call the police," yelled one.

"They gotta stop that guy," said another.

Somebody brought a six-pack of beer and the conversation turned to a party. Beer was more important than drawing attention. Some "smoke" on the side was available too but you could not have police or fire around for this kind of party.

The arsonist was now angry. "These damn hotdog heroes got to stop!"

Having failed to get his lover's attention, determination set in and he added more gasoline. Four times he lit the fire. Four times the hotdog team, including the building manager/owner, put out the fire.

The fifth and final time the arsonist's rage had grown from mad to monstrous.

*He would finally get it right! He would teach this woman a lesson!*

Squeezing the gas can handle, he poured fuel as he walked from one end of the upstairs hall to the other. The old shag carpet released the vapor and filled the hall behind him. He struck the match, pitched it and ran like a hoodlum.

He had finally gotten the nerve to kill with no regard for the path of destruction he would leave behind.

The flames rose from the carpet swaying like a Kansas wheat field in high winds. Fire licked the sides of the walls and worked its way to the attic. Once the fire spread to the attic, it raced in every direction. The resident cavalry roared again, but this time the fire was too big, too hot, too out of control and too dangerous. People scurried to hit the fire alarms. Nothing worked. They tried to get out but the broken furniture blocked the path. Some screamed, some hid, and some were too old and handicapped to get out. Some found a phone and called 911.

"Hurry! Fire . . . fire . . . fire!" Frantic callers begged and pleaded with dispatcher to, "Send the fire department now! Please hurry, the building is on fire! Please hurry!"

Having served as an emergency dispatcher, I remember those frenzied and terrified calls. "We are on the way," I tried to assure as I wiped the sweat from the palm of my hands.

A verbal alert was sounded, "Tell the troops to pull up their boots."

Pull up your boots meant, "You got one." Back before bunker pants, I had ¾ boots that folded down. During a fire, we pulled up our boots to cover and protect the upper part of our legs.

The sun rose early for the Dallas Fire Department, Tuesday morning, August 13, 1996. While 911 telecommunication specialists feverishly took emergency calls, Engine 46's siren was screaming up South R. L. Thornton Freeway, unknowingly headed toward the kind of life-threatening emergency we were prepared for—but hoped we never had to experience.

One lieutenant, a twenty-six-year veteran, was riding the seat on Engine 46 that night. All his years of training, leadership and experience were going to be challenged in a way usually only found in textbooks. The engine topped the hill near Laureland, and the fire lit up the horizon. In route, the lieutenant put two alarms on the fire. As Engine 46 pulled up on the scene, the lieutenant began to see the real nature of the incident.

"People were jumping out of windows everywhere. One lady jumped out the second story window and landed right in front of our engine! We could not even make our way over to help her, because another lady came up and started screaming, 'My baby is right up there.' She pointed above his head to the second floor."

The now-awake security guard chimed in, "There are a bunch of old people right up there." He also pointed up to the second floor.

Engine 46 passed command and began a quick attack on the fire, the goal being to rescue those trapped in the upper rooms. They quickly laid a line moved up the stairs and toward the fire.

Paramedics were already pulling people out, fire licking behind them from the windows. Nearly all personnel arriving were catching jumpers or babies being tossed to them from above.

The three men of Engine 46 battled the blaze toward room identified as having a child trapped, but within twenty-five feet of reaching the room, they ran out of hose. The room appeared darkened, but fire was everywhere above in the attic.

The lieutenant instructed his men to cover him with the hose line. He crawled alone toward the fire to the room where a child lay motionless.

He entered the room and patted his hands toward the location of the bed and almost immediately felt flesh.

"It was a miracle I found her so fast," he recalled later.

It was her leg. He tugged gently and heard a breath or groan or gush of air.

"It was hard to tell if it was a breath or not, I thought she still might be alive," the lieutenant recounted.

He crawled to her side and removed his facemask and covered the child's face. Quickly picking her up he raced toward safety, all the while gasping and inhaling thick black smoke. The hallway floor had burned through and he fell feeling a sharp pain in his legs and butt. He crawled out of the hole, rose again ignoring the pain in his own body, determined to finish the job he started.

Once outside he handed off the child to paramedics and returned to face the hellhole again. One rescue after another, hitting it hard without rest. Other crews jumped in and firefighters were literally dragging people out one at a time. Elderly, children, parents, and workers trapped by the fire were saved. The men and women of Dallas Fire Department moved those that could not move themselves. Miracle after miracle went down that night, and I witnessed it all.

*Amazing miracles!*

This is only one of many stories of rescue, challenge and courage shown that night. Nearly every member of the Dallas Fire Department who arrived rescued a person from this incident.

It was a night when I felt proud to be a member of this department. This was a night when firefighters reached beyond themselves and showed authentic love—the ultimate sacrifice we can make toward one another.

*I am so proud of the love the Bubbas have for people.*

When making the rounds, I finally caught up with the crew of Engine 46 at the canteen. I asked the lieutenant to tell me what had happened. A moment after completing his story, he asked the dreaded question.

"Did the little girl make it?"

There was an immediate bond that is formed between rescuers and their victims. The lieutenant's sense of caring was proof that this bond existed here also.

"Uh . . . lieutenant . . . no. She did not make it. She died at the hospital."

It was easy to see he was going through that all too familiar and unsettling things we rescuers go through when we struggle and lose—we deal with it quietly.

Then after a brief moment, the lieutenant picked up his mask and marched back toward the fire. He still had a job to do.

Going into battle, each firefighter's face displayed a look of *faith on fire* and each were willing to take the dare and rise to the challenge offered by this monster conflagration. There was no question about it. We all gutted it up and did what had to be done. At this moment, I realized I was among the best of the best in the fire service.

In all, EMS processed hundreds of patients. Out of hundreds, only twenty-three had to be transported due to injuries from jumping out windows. Everyone else suffered emotional trauma from the event.

Our chaplain's presence at the scene was a welcome sight, not only to the personnel he supported, but also to the citizens who witnessed the horrifying event. Many families with children were first on the scene, because they were the first to escape. This escape was made with only the clothes on their back and the children they held tightly in their arms. They stood still, watching the fire, mostly silent. Apprehension, fear and relief etched onto their faces.

Victims crammed under the cover of the old, shut down gas station next door to the motel. The wooden fence around the service station served as a fire barrier. People appeared to hide behind the fence as if still needing protection from the fire.

The thousand-mile stare we often hear about in Critical Incident Stress training made its unwelcome appearance.

There was one lady I will never forget. I thought she was going to explode emotionally as she shared her version of the story. In front of the media's cameras, her eyes grew wide with panicked excitement, as if you could see right through to her frightened soul. Every sentence drained her strength, and she wavered and labored with each breath. She swallowed hard. You could tell it hurt. With eyes wide as saucers, she tried to hold back the flood of frightened tears pushing their way through her already moistened eyelids.

"They were trying to get out"

(*Huh, huh*).

"They screamed and screamed."

(*Huh, huh*).

"Oh God, there was nothing we could do."

(*Huh, huh*).

"The children—Oh God, the children. They saw it all."

(*Huh, huh*).

"It was horrible; we did not know what to do." Her head dropped from exhaustion, as every word uttered was emotionally excruciating. I stroked her back trying to slow her hyperventilation.

*Big Mamma would give a hug at this moment.*

Never sure if it is the right thing to do, I put my arms around her, held her tight and let her sob into my shoulder. Hugs do not take away pain, but they somehow temporarily short-circuit agony. The camera lights went out, and she and I stood there just holding on to one another. It was a moment in time, a snapshot of something hard to explain.

We were two opposites. I was from the north side of town, and she was from the south. Together we shared in something awful and wonderful. Not the color of our skin, not the amount of money we had in our pockets, not the stories we carried in our minds—nothing else mattered. We stood there and held on to one another unified in agony. Finally, a chaplain came by, and I released her to his tender care. There was more work for me to do.

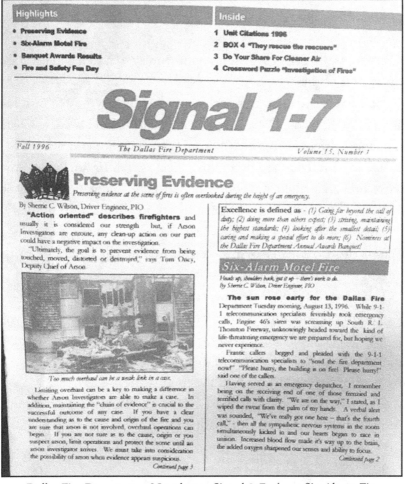

Dallas Fire Department Newsletter, Signal 1-7, about Six-Alarm Fire

It was just a matter of time before this massive and hostile inferno began to surrender its incandescent glory to our firefighters. We had attacked it from all sides. Ladder pipes were set for a surround and drown. Firefighters had that rough and dirty look about them. There was soot mixed with sweat-covered faces.

In teams, they made their way to the canteen to quench their thirst. I watched them curiously. Water and Gatorade were always coldest at this point. Some men dropped to their knees in pure exhaustion, too tired to even remove their hot bunker gear. This was one proud moment for the Dallas Fire Department. This was when we worked together and created miracles over and over. I could not wait to write this story.

Serving as the PIO, gave me an opportunity to watch and learn from the very best of the best.

The owners and operators of the motel, as well as the arsonist, faced charges brought by the Dallas Fire Department, Arson Division. Owners and operators were charged with criminal negligence and homicide for not meeting fire code requirements, such as: failure to report any of the five fires that night to the fire department, screwing/locking shut exit doors, and allowing smoke detectors to be disabled. In spite of this being an arson fire, the Dallas Fire Department felt that the owners and operators of the motel caused the death of a female child due to their disregard for fire life safety standards.

On August 22, 1996, the alleged arsonist was arrested.

The letter nominating the lieutenant for an award was easy to write. Not only did he receive an award from the Dallas Fire Department that year, *Firehouse* magazine gave him the prestigious Medal of Valor. I wish more firefighters could have told me their stories.

The men and women of the Dallas Fire Department are good at creating miracles in the face of madness.

*It only takes a little faith on fire.*

## Super Bowl XXVII

Super Bowl XXVII was played on January 31, 1993, in Pasadena, California. The Dallas Cowboys defeated the Buffalo Bills. Troy Aikman, quarterback for the Cowboys, had been named Super Bowl MVP. Aikman completed 20+ passes and four touchdowns.

Fast-forward to February 10, 1993. The beginning of that day was a great day in Dallas. People were gathered for the parade to celebrate the Cowboys win at the Super Bowl. I was on loan to the city manager's office, serving as the City of Dallas Public Information Officer.

It was freezing outside. I was headed to City Hall to put out a press release on a fire. After exiting Woodall Rodgers Freeway, I turned left onto Griffin and passed by Fire Station 18, noticing it was empty. Looking up toward downtown Dallas, I saw all the craziness the media would talk about for the next month.

People were pouring in and out of downtown. Traffic was at a standstill. I saw some kids throw something at a bus. It splattered across the bus window. The person attempting to get on the bus was dragged backwards, but he struggled loose, ran to the bus, the driver opened the door, let him in and took off. You could tell by the look on the bus driver's face, he was scared and wanted to vacate the area. The group of kids who dragged the person backward laughed.

*Hmm . . . a pocket of troublemakers on such a great day of celebration.*

Looking across the street, I saw a young man waving a handgun. He wore a satisfied and fiendish grin. There were a few officers up ahead, but their hands were full with the crowd. The disturbance was growing rapidly by the minute. The young man pointed the gun at an older female and pretended to pull the trigger. She screamed and ducked. Now I was scared.

"DALLAS—A downtown celebration by about 400,000 Dallas Cowboy fans dissolved into sporadic violence Tuesday as police attempted to control surging crowds."

*—Associated Press*

The kids with the gunman laughed at his antics. Some of the group seemed to be under the influence, most likely alcohol because walking straight seem a challenge. One kid was trying to help another who was stumbling. As I moved closer into downtown, the scene intensified.

*Impossible!*

People were fighting, throwing things, cursing and mad as hell. Never had I seen the streets of Dallas so out of control. This was not a threat—it was a full-blown riot.

The police were out-numbered. They drew their batons and held them up attempting to make their arms longer to hold back the crowds. The parade moved from the west to the east through downtown. I was forced to turn west and cut through the West End of downtown. As I inched my way toward city hall, the mayhem surrounded me.

The police were overwhelmed with rioters around the bus station and the hamburger joint on Commerce. One lone officer stood with his hands out to order people to stand back. Someone shoved the officer and the crowd broke free. They all took off running up Commerce chasing after the parade.

"Violence erupted on every street corner in about a 10-block area. Kids out of school and unsupervised vandalized stores, mugged innocent bystanders, battled with cops, and even fought each other."
—WFAA Staff, WFAA.com

Finally I worked my way over to City Hall and it was locked down. So I drove to the Dallas Convention Center and took cover in the underground parking.

More than two-dozen people were taken to area hospitals as fights broke out among fans. There was at least one incident of gunfire and several stabbings. The absenteeism rate at several Dallas independent schools was reportedly in excess of 60 percent.

So, the Cowboys won, and Dallas celebrated.

Today was an impossible day, but a miracle day all wrapped up into a shift because no firefighters were injured.

# Chapter 8

---

# SMOLDERING PHASE

Definition: A steady burning phase where flames may cease to exist if the area of confinement is sufficiently airtight. Burning reduced to glowing embers.

"If you don't stand for something, you will fall for anything."

—Anonymous

## Recruiter

Nothing could have prepared me for the hostility to come in my new assignment. It was my task to select sixty new applicants for two upcoming rookie classes. I was told there were approximately 250 applicants from which to choose. The applications were kept manually in file folders. Our staff had to read massive amounts of paperwork and manually pick the best candidates. There had to be a better way. Being action-oriented and organized, I wanted to correct those problems. As the new recruiter for the department, I quickly realized there were problems with the hiring procedures.

To solve this overwhelming problem, I created a database and entered each applicant's information, including the key college requirements for the job and their test scores from the civil service exam.

When finished with the database, a simple report revealed there were more than 420 white applicants, sixty Black applicants, thirty Hispanic applicants and a few female applicants. We now had a baseline from which to work. When I sorted them by scores, the choice for best applicants became clear. However, this did not fit into the minority percentages dictated by my supervisor.

My supervisor, a civilian, explained the hiring percentages were one-third Black, one-third Hispanic, and of course, any women if possible. Any leftover slots might be filled with white males as long as there was one minority for each Anglo hired. I agreed with this plan right up until we ran out of qualified minority applicants and were sitting on a great bunch of people who were capable of doing the job, but simply did not have the right skin color.

*Where is the integrity in discrimination?*

The budget required sixty applicants be hired, and I only had thirty-eight at the minority one-to-one ratio. We had already used every available minority applicant that successfully completed the process. With twenty-two positions still available, I wanted to hire the balance with whoever was qualified. I pulled the top rated candidates which were all white from the database and asked to present them for consideration.

*Big mistake! They did not have the right skin color to be hired.*

The department was paying about *two million dollars in overtime.* We needed to hire, hire, and hire *like we were on fire*! My opinion to fill the position with qualified applicants caused friction, dissension, and a backlash in my direction.

*I am wrapped in my own annoyance. This is not right!*

At first I thought the problem in the office was because personnel were not familiar with the computer database. Making an effort to train them was met with high resistance.

*People do not like change, especially when it foils their plan to discriminate.*

And, there was an undercurrent of something else.

*Does being a good old gal mean looking the other way when something is wrong?*

My boss stood over me late one afternoon while I was working on the database and asked, "Can I trust you?"

I sat quietly looking at him, my mind racing as to what he was referring to, and I nodded my head yes.

*No matter how persuasive, I am always defending my view.*

The database was simple. You could sort the candidates by any criteria desired. I thought it should be based on their grades and test scores, not on race or gender. The database was guilty of objectively documenting discrimination based on skin color.

> "He [my supervisor] was concerned because fire department personnel were scrutinized by a multitude of people and worried that if the proverbial [#&%] would hit the fan—Wilson would go back to the fire station, and he would go home."
>
> —Dallas Observer

Although I seriously questioned the legality of the quota system, I continued to do the job and met the quota percentages as best I could—not to do so meant I would be insubordinate.

*If I did not follow orders, I was insubordinate. If I did follow orders, I was discriminating. I do not know what to do.*

My supervisor and co-worker had to get rid of the database because it proved discrimination, and that meant getting rid of me.

*Racial and gender flavor stirred my life again.*

Another problem was scheduling lie detector test for candidates. We did not have enough of the required testers to take on our volume of applicants, so minorities went first and the others waited. This exam became the bottleneck in recruiting and we were lucky to get two people tested a week. When the class did not fill up, you guessed it—it was my fault.

*We do not have the resources to meet our goals—somebody has to take the blame, and it was me. Impossible! I have been set up to fail.*

Having told the chief of training well in advance of the problem, I shared the secret of what was hindering the hiring process. This chief had some pull and he pushed for applicants that had completed the process. When the chief of training demanded that my supervisor deliver the candidates we were sitting on, my supervisor went nuts. His anger rained down on me nearly every moment of every single day.

When the supervisor had asked me if he could trust me, he meant could *he* trust me. I said yes, and I meant that *my department and my coworkers* could trust me to do the right thing. Perceptions are really our own interpretations of things.

*My integrity was not for sale, and I did not want to be a party to discrimination.*

Later, during a tour of Civil Service, I was introduced to the department head. By way of conversation, she shared her ideas on how to increase the applicant pool. I was interested and listened and my coworker reported the conversation to my supervisor, and he went ballistic again.

*I despise screamers.*

"You don't set policy," he said in two decibels louder than normal.

"What are you referring to?"

"Your conversation with the department head of Civil Service," he spouted off.

"I was introduced to her. I was cordial. I listened to her. What do you want me to do?"

"Your conversation turned policy and you are not allowed to set policy," he barked.

"I was not in control of the conversation. She is a department head and can talk about what she wants to."

*Why do we need to hide anything?*

The behavior toward me had become more than unacceptable. He screamed regularly and in a violent tone.

*No team dynamics or mutual respect to be found here. I long to go back to the station and be tied to a tree or have a bucket of water dumped on my head.*

Now he took it one step further. My supervisor opened his pocketknife, smiled devilishly and began to pick at his nails. "You will obey. You will not attempt to set policy! Understood?"

"Yes sir," I said with more gumption than I felt.

*He likes to control women!*

Walking away, I felt confused and attacked. It apparently did not matter what I did, my opinion was useless and this man was now out to get me.

*What was the pocketknife about? Intimidation? Is he for real?*

In August I was once again in my supervisor's office discussing candidates and looming deadlines. As I stood in front of his desk, he sat behind it waiting to pounce. An assistant stuck her head in the door said something regarding a "Clarence." She promptly left the room.

Media had recently relived the Clarence Thomas and Anita Hill fiasco on television.

I questioned, "Thomas?"

Clarence Thomas was an associate justice of the Supreme Court of the United States. Anita Hill was an attorney and academic professor who accused U.S. Supreme Court nominee Clarence Thomas, who was her supervisor at the U.S. Department of Education, of sexual harassment. What was going on in recruiting with my supervisor and me mirrored this controversy, except it was workplace violence and not sexual harassment.

My supervisor reached in his pocket and pulled his knife again. He opened it with a snap of his wrist. He looked directly at me and pointed with his knife, "Don't be talking about my man."

A police officer told me once a person has a knife, watch his eyes. The eyes will tell you his next move.

I maintained eye contact.

*His eyes scare the hell out of me!*

He repeated his warning while starring daggers at me and waving the knife in short slicing strokes.

*Stand up to his def-con level 5 tantrum. Do not be afraid!*

Glaring directly into those ominous eyes I gutted it up and I said, "I have had people on the ambulance pull knives on me before . . ."

Again, I was interrupted again with "Don't be talking about my man" and he made the slicing motion again.

*Oh, God! He is serious! I wish someone else were here to witness this.*

Feeling threatened, I turned and left the room.

*Surely not! How can a department operate this way?*

Worried, I tried not to jump to conclusions and assume the worst, but I did. I began to walk ever so softly around this man. I withdrew.

*Nobody should have to live this way! Stay calm. Write it all down.*

A few weeks later, while discussing some candidates, my supervisor snapped out, "I guess I am going to have to pull my knife again."

*No, he just did not! He was not kidding! He was threatening me! He thinks he can bully me!* His words angered me and struck a chord of fear. Again, I quickly changed the subject and left his office.

*Why did he feel a need to threaten me?*

Doing exactly what he asked me to do, I could not understand his hatred toward me, other than I was a strong woman not willing to coward down to him. Nothing we were discussing had any emotional essence to it, nor did he seem angry about anything when he said it. I was making notes of the event and decided to use the holiday weekend to think it over and discuss the incident with my husband.

There was another issue I was facing. My supervisor's signature was required for me to get the captain-level pay. Prior to my arriving in recruiting, my subordinate had received captain's pay—he never missed a lick of it. Since I outranked him, I was to receive the captain's assignment pay.

*It was not that much money. It was the principal of it. Pay him, but not pay me?*

After many months of failing to pay me repeatedly, I filed a grievance.

*Why am I such a fighter? God why did you make me this way?*

Suddenly my *faith on fire* burned about as bright as a birthday candle.

The final blow was the day he handed me a letter of counseling which accused me of violating city rules governing unacceptable conduct. He stated I had not followed written or verbal discussions when I was introduced to the department head of Civil Service.

*So, there is a rule for introductions now? He is worried I will expose the illegal activity of discrimination? Well, he is right about that—I will expose this!*

Within the year, the fire department investigated my complaints, but took no action.

*Impossible!*

This little incident exposed the department. So to keep the peace, the letter was removed from my file and dropped. I was moved to the academy to train rookies. I felt somewhat betrayed by the department, and I was sorely disappointed.

*Discrimination continued.*

That was not good enough for my supervisor, though he wanted more. He continued to appear at my work place with his little knife. Never saying or doing anything, just making sure that I was aware—I was still on his mind.

*He has now upped the game from agitation to harassment and persecution along with his few well-placed shots at me.*

With the stress of not being believed, not being paid appropriately, being transferred and continually harassed, I was at my lowest.

The flame of my faith flickered.

*Pushing through the pain is what separates the winners from the losers.*

The certainty of purpose I had always lived with, now turned to frustration, and the idea of giving up on this job presented itself to me again. I took a medical leave of absence to heal and recover.

During this time, I reflected on my years of service, the battles I had to fight as the first female in the department.

*Had it been worth the cost? What about the time away from my family, physical stress and strain, and mental anguish?*

Should I leave the job I had come to love? Was it somebody else's turn to fight?

"'I love the department, and I plan on staying a long time,' I told a reporter. 'But I'm a fighter. I have been injured in fires. I have had knives pulled on me in the back of ambulances. I have had guys not like me. I dealt with all of it. It was part of the job. But what happened to me when I went to recruiting was just something I could not deal with. I was made to look like a problem child, and that is not true. It was unfair, and it was ugly. I really believe it was all about power and race.'"

—Dallas Observer

My life was infused with racial flavor and it tasted bitter. As part of the department's future, I wanted to take a stand for a department with no racial or gender issues. My sense of right and wrong was somehow skewed according to this man. If it was skewed, I could not see it. I wanted no discrimination, period. No discrimination against anyone.

*Race and gender issues continue to flavor my life.*

While thinking and recovering, a sense of purpose welled up inside me. Take a stand for others. This was nothing new, but it was tainted with overwhelming problems and fear.

*How could I have changed this?*

My responsibility lay somewhere between forcing and controlling what I thought was right in contrast to being loving and focusing on unity no matter what or who I faced.

My supervisor in recruiting was right about one thing, he did go home, and I returned to the fire station.

*Life and death are in the power of your words.*

It was disappointing that our department had its dirty little secrets. But even more so, I was saddened by my own lack of love for those with whom I disagreed.

While taking time off, I was confronted with finishing my career. With a little time, forethought and faith, I prayed.

My mom realized I was hurting and depressed. She had given me the book on the prayer of Jabez. I read it over and over. Severely humbled, I returned to work.

> "Now Jabez called on the God of Israel, saying, 'Oh that You would bless me indeed and enlarge my border, and that Your hand might be with me, and that You would keep me from harm that it may not pain me!' And God granted him what he requested."
>
> —1 Chronicles 4:10, NIV

I am lucky our God is a forgiving God. I needed forgiveness.

## Flashover Exercise

On March 23, 1999, I was setting up an exercise to teach a rookie class. We were about to sweat out all the poisons of past sins in the flashover container.

When organic materials are heated, they undergo thermal decomposition and release flammable gases. A flashover is the simultaneous ignition of combustible material in an enclosed area. To the untrained eye it could look like the air is exploding and on fire.

Since flashovers are potentially fatal events, recognizing the signs of this phenomena and equipping members with survival techniques was paramount. This training is challenging and tests firefighters resolve, stamina and courage.

As the instructor, my job was to produce several rollovers and flashovers so firefighters could learn to read the signs of a potential flashover. It was crucial all firefighters realized that during an actual emergency the techniques demonstrated were to be used only once, because they only allowed the firefighter about five seconds to escape before the flashover. Escape was typically only possible if a firefighter was five feet or less from an exit.

This training is dangerous, and it requires several instructors at various points inside the container. A safety officer is also required to double check the correct donning of all turnout gear to prevent potential injuries and to monitor all activity during this training.

When a fire is in its growth stage, you can see sporadic flashes of flame mixed with smoke referred to as rollovers or fire snakes. A rollover is a warning sign of a potential flashover. The cause of flashover is credited to excessive buildup of heat. As the fire burns, the gas contents are heated to ignition temperature. The fire flashes then the fire gases erupt simultaneously (flashing) and become fully involved in fire.

A flashover is more common today than in the past, partly due to the fact that firefighters rarely find single pane glass windows anymore. Single panes become molten and runny, venting themselves easily, while double panes and treated windows used in today's structures simply hold in the heat creating super-heated smoke that flashes quickly.

In the flashover container, firefighters are able to watch and study the fire as it grows. As the thermal intensity increases fire will release rollovers that mimic multi-dimensional fiery snakes. The fiery snakes reach out away and above the fire like rolling, moving fingers. When firefighters see this fire activity we prepare for possible flashover.

Nozzle techniques called *penciling* are used. Penciling is quick burst of water aimed at the ceiling above the fire. Penciling helps maintain thermal balance temporarily. It does not drown the fire. These tactics may delay flashover long enough to give firefighters extra seconds needed to escape.

If a firefighter is caught inside a potential flashover, we hunker down low and direct the nozzle toward the ceiling and fan the spray wide, creating a curtain of water between us and fire—kind of like an umbrella protects you during rain. It is our last chance of surviving. This is risky and used only as a last resort and does not ensure success.

Holding off starting the fire in the flashover container, we ogled and eyed the heavy smoke coming from a building just south of downtown. The rookies asked if we could go to the fire.

"We might go, if it goes to five alarms," I announced.

We warned the rookies that they would only be picking up hose and backing up the firefighters. They would not fight fire.

Extra alarms started rolling in as fast as fire communications could dispatch. With a rapid-fire escalation, the fire went to three-alarms, four-alarms, five-alarms and then six-alarms. Within minutes I had the rookies gathered with their bunker gear and we headed for a passenger van. In route, the fire went to seven-alarms.

## Seven-Alarm Fire

Without flashing lights or screaming sirens to get our pulses racing, we moseyed our way toward downtown. We had loaded up in a fifteen-passenger van to transport the rookies to the fire. There was nothing exciting about this code 1 drive (without lights or sirens) to psych me up to fight fire, like when riding an apparatus responding, code 3. I had no idea I was on my way to the biggest blaze of my career. Experience proved it was not likely that we would get to fight any fire or have any real fun today. I relaxed.

While reporting in at the command post I heard a few muffled explosions. It felt like the ground below us was grumbling. The rookies' eyes grew wide with excitement, and I have to admit, so did mine.

Hose lines were stretched all around the north side of the building, and the runoff water was so hot you could feel it through your boots—like walking through a lake of fire.

Chief Baker was the incident commander. Having stood by his side in these kinds of events before, I knew there was no time for social graces. I just nodded and he nodded back.

*A silent alarm went off in my head. He does not usually wear such a grim face.*

Not only was a sizable portion of this commercial building involved in fire, but also the situation was becoming ever more challenging in that the materials burning were producing enormous amounts of thick black smoke. The smoke was so poisonous, it required evacuation of the neighborhoods north and east of the fire as the wind was out of the southwest.

I was ordered to take my group of rookies and report to the back of the fire to assist a truck crew in breaking down its five-inch hose. We had to quickly back out the ladder truck set next to the fire or risk damaging it—retreating.

When walking around to the back of the building, I heard the order over the radio, "All firefighters evacuate the building. We are going to a defensive operation." The warning was repeated several times, and the high-low siren sounded as another warning to all firefighters to get out.

*Impossible! We just showed up at the biggest structure fire of my career and we were already backing out!*

Offensive firefighting is challenging like dancing with the devil. This is where we bury up inside with the fire and push it out of the building. Defensive firefighting means we pull out of the building and set ladder pipes keeping the devil contained to the building. Basically, it means we are giving up the building and protecting the surroundings.

The block-long building located on Gould Street just south of downtown Dallas housed a company that recycled rubber and plastics. The building was U-shaped with a courtyard in the middle. At one end of the building was the processing area, and the other end was a warehouse. In between the two ends of the building were various offices and storage areas.

The fire started in the processing end of the building located on the north side. As we made our way around to the back of the fire, one fire truck was positioned up inside the courtyard and another was in the alleyway behind the warehouse. Both trucks had been positioned to utilize their water towers for a *surround and drown* operation, but the fire grew so fast and radiated so much heat that the trucks had to be relocated or risk damage.

One thing I had to admit about working for the Dallas Fire Recue Department was we always had excellent equipment. The idea of burning up not one, but two pieces of million-dollar equipment would be a horrible ordeal.

*Now I understand why the chief had such a grim face.*

Once we disconnected the hose lines and rescued one truck, we moved over to the second truck and backed it out too. We were told to hold our position at the back of the fire.

Another academy instructor took a Halligan tool and forcibly pried open a small side door to the warehouse portion of the building. We stood peeping inside the warehouse—the dark bowels of hell on earth. Crackles and pops were heard in the ceiling.

*You can't see it, but the beast is already here.*

The warehouse was a huge, two-story room filled with small round chips of black and green rubber, possibly pieces of tires. This fire load was made up of mounds of this product, most of them six feet high or higher. There were a few colossal mounds as high as the ceiling that appeared to have been dropped through a hopper on top of the building. The warehouse was a gigantic open structure. This was a perfect meal for a hungry fire beast, and I could already hear its stomach growling. Our torment would be this fire's amusement. This was not just a fire, this was an out-of-control monster. It was present and ready and daring us to face it.

Any firefighter that says he or she does not have some amount of fear when facing a behemoth conflagration, is a liar. But it is not about having fear; it is about facing your fear, especially when facing a huge fire. Being determined and declaring victory no matter how big the infernos rein our everyday lives takes courage too. We all stood there curious, facing the exceedingly fierce and enormous demon. We were interested yet apprehensive.

*Firefighters revealed a winning attitude of faith on fire. Oh boy, this is gonna be entertaining.*

When serving as the chief's incident command technician, I always tried to anticipate what the commanders were going to do. I compared my thoughts with theirs, and sometimes we would discuss events afterward and how they played out. Today, facing this fire, I no longer wanted to play this guessing game. I was happy to fall back into the field of yellow coats and helmets and follow orders. I still had lessons to learn.

A few years before, I had seen the movie *Back draft* with the Bubbas off-duty. We made fun of how movie magic created a fire with such a killer personality. I have always respected fire's power and force but, until today, I had never experienced this level of violence or explosive personality. Today, fighting fire took on a whole new perspective—fighting with the demons from the underworld.

The fire relentlessly slammed its way through the building causing us to back up each time we attempted to stop it with our defensive attack. Our first attempt to stop was in the processing area. The fire turned and headed for the south side of the structure. Firefighters would draw a new line in the sand and the demon stepped over it like one hundred thousand soldiers, marching in unison, lifting their legs high and daring us to stand in its way. There was literally nothing we could do to stop it.

*Finally, I am facing an impossible fire!*

Command ordered us (the two rookie teams) to lay two 2 ½ inch lines with straight bore nozzles on the south end of the warehouse. There were so many demands on our department during this fire; rookie teams were placed in service as an external fire attack team.

*Unbelievable!*

One of the rookies raised his arms straight in the air like an Olympian saying, "Yeah, we are gonna get to squirt some water!"

One of the other instructors told him, "Put your arms down and shut up, or you will wait for us in the van."

We laid our heavy caliber lines in the backyard of a house that butted up against the south end of the warehouse. The building occupied an entire block of land. We were our department's last defense between the warehouse, connecting the neighborhood and the backyard of two tiny houses. We waited for the fire dragon to work its way past the real firefighters, and show up so the rookies could have a little action.

Once the fire flashed inside the warehouse, propane tanks inside the structure exploded. It sounded as though the beast was beating its chest declaring victory, then we heard a loud whoosh. The building vibrated and quivered.

Although the fire had yet to show itself through the roof, we needed to be further back to protect us from the dragon's breath and radiant heat, but all the space we had available were those two backyards. The hotter the fire got the more determined we became to protect these two little exposures that stood as the gateway into the neighborhood. Looks of determination came over the rookies' faces—just what we needed to see. I smiled.

When firefighting gets in your blood, you rise to the challenge, facing the dragon with determination. *Faith on fire* becomes a way of being for firefighters.

We heard the air horn alert. Water was coming. The engineer opened the gate valve and the hose began to fill. The hose straightened itself out and then began to snake around the backyard out of control with rookies hanging on for dear life. I have to admit, I found the sight funny, but then jumped in to help them wrestle the powerful hose to the ground. I radioed for the driver-engineer to drop the pressure. It took a little time and a lot of muscle to get that pulsating and bulging line under control. Managing this hose was more like attempting to bend a hefty wooden beam. I guessed that the driver-engineer was using that all too familiar philosophy we seem to rely on: *big fire, big pressure*. Hoping to maintain better control, we managed to loop the line into a 360°circle, then directed the nozzle toward the south end of the warehouse and waited for the fire-demon to emerge.

Once the fire got a good bite on the warehouse, we started to see thick black plumes of smoke rising above our heads. The fire was working its way in our direction. The smoke puffed, blew, belched and sucked in every direction imaginable and finally the fire-devil screamed a warning announcing its arrival—then the fire showed itself in an array of dancing colors—red, orange, white, blue.

When the fire first broke through the south eave of the warehouse, it wickedly licked and lapped up the sides toward the roofline. It danced a war dance in our direction while consuming parts of the roof. Blasphemous language came spewing with a thunderous roar. It was expressing extreme hatred for all who stood in its way.

Slapped by our straight bore nozzles flooding its mouth, the fire withdrew, regrouped and came again and again and again, each time dazzling us with a sparkling array of fireworks. With a vengeance and roaring like a lion, the cat rushed for its prey. We shot at the king of his pride with heavy streams of water and momentarily stopped its roar. The radiant heat pawed back at us and clawed our gear. I hunkered down hiding my face inside my collar to keep the torrid heat from burning my airway.

Fighting the nozzle reaction in a mud puddle caused by the overspray did not help our defensive situation either. Our bodies were glued to the hose line, but as a team we managed to hold on. If the hose line ever got away from us, it would have hammered us to death.

Trying to get in a comfortable position, I wrapped my legs around the hose, leaned back to relieve the strain on my back, and waited for more fire to march our way.

What seemed like only minutes ago, I was going to teach the rookies all I knew about flashover. Now with a twisted set of events, I am next to my rookies, facing the biggest flashing fire of my career, all while wrestling a rebellious hose and holding on for dear life. With twenty-plus years of experience, I was as much a student of this massive firestorm as any new rookie.

Repeatedly, the fire teased us with moments of violent raging, then sucked back only to spew and spit and gallop head-on toward us again. The energy behind the raging inferno was explosive. Suddenly the smoke and fire appeared above our heads and hovered like a vile genie just released from its bottle. This fiery giant shrouded in black smoke opened its mouth and coughed, hacked and sneezed its threats in our direction with a thunderous roar. We ducked to avoid this monster's hot breath spitting directly at us. The superheated air choked and tightened our airways. Fear bound itself around us like a snake constricting its prey, but we held on with our *faith on fire.*

Sweeping the fire back and forth with our line only complicated our efforts. We were now sliding ankle deep in a massive mud puddle, created from overspray and spewing steam. It was as though the water from our hose line was hitting a brick wall and bouncing back at us in the form of a steam shower. It was punishing. There was no place to back up and failure was not an option.

*Impossible!*

With a distinctive malicious presence, the penetrating heat of the fire beat us down. The air was now filled with black muck and an oxygen-depleted atmosphere. It was exhausting just to try and get a breath. I desperately longed for a drink or even just a drop of cool water. It was as if God had left us alone in the seventh level of hell. This demonic creature from below was pleased to welcome us and slammed violently in our direction again.

We were just outside the danger of the collapse zone, but suddenly the small alley, a few scorched trees, and the chain link fence between the fire and us took on an eerie tomb-like feeling. Skin under our full turnout gear felt as though it would slough off any minute.

This kind of heat can only be compared to that of a three-dimensional jet fuel, a lake of fire where we march and sway the nozzle back and forth. During that kind of fuel fire it was like walking through bubbling mud from the abyss. You felt like the skin on your feet was peeling off one layer at a time through your boots. At times it is so punishing I wanted to give up. But holding our position in the face of the impossible is what firefighters and paramedics do.

We begged again for another line with a fog nozzle so we could fan it out like a curtain for protection from the radiant heat. The line never showed. In the face of this impossible fire, we held our position.

More muffled explosions and fireworks went off in the sky closer above our heads. We titled our heads all the way back to watch amazed at the violence, then quickly ducked our chin inside our coat collar for fear the sight would leave us burned and scared.

The fire flashed to one side of the roofline, and we knocked it down. Then it flashed on the other side, and we knocked it down again. This fire was like a caged animal looking for an escape route, and each time it attempted escape it was met with a slap from our two straight bore nozzles. The more we slapped the fire, the angrier the creature grew.

"When you pass through the waters, I will be with you; and when you pass through the rivers, they will not sweep over you. When you walk through the fire, you will not be burned the flames will not set you ablaze."

—Isaiah 43:2–3, NIV

The giant stopped and snorted like a bull headed for a matador and then finally, as if settling its score with us, it busted through and consumed the entire roof of the warehouse. The ravenous appetite of this bull was not satisfied and pitiful screams from the building became louder and louder. Over the course of many hours the corrugated metal building became superheated. The metal stretched, elongated and began to bend, give and groan. We hit the molten metal with water, and it would sizzle and shriek and spit steam in agony.

Letting out loud agonizing and haunting groans, pieces of the building began to fold under its own weight. Slowly, the building surrendered and screeched to a halt, collapsed. It lay in a huge pile of liquefied metal on top of mounds of bubbling rubber and plastic surrounded by an insatiable lake of fire.

*We won in the face of the impossible!*

After about five hours of fighting this fire, a chief came around and asked us if we had taken a break. We were forgotten because we were not a responding unit assigned to the fire.

"No, we haven't had a break, but could really use one," was my response as my leg and back muscles were beginning to cramp.

Replacement companies soon arrived and the rookies all hopped up and dashed to the canteen like kids running for the tree on Christmas morning. We older, more mature, firefighter instructors, boot-scooted our way to the canteen genteelly. When we got there, there was not anything left to eat.

Box 4, our canteen volunteers, had brought in plenty of drinks and food, but citizens evacuated from the area came up and ate all the food. There was only water and coffee left. We gulped down a few cups of water and sat down to rest. Before our break was over, relief companies showed up and thankfully, we headed back to the academy.

In route back, all the instructors agreed that we had never faced fire with such a violent personality. The rookies were thrilled. I was thrilled.

"It was a spectacular fire!" said, one. They were so excited they sounded like ten-year-olds at their first fireworks show.

One of the instructors told them, "This is as good as ever it gets."

Firefighters remained in a hydraulic overhaul operation for days, and the thick black smoke continued to rise in massive amounts. It was such heavy smoke that the Environmental Protection Agency (EPA) showed up at the scene. I wondered what they thought they could do to make a difference. I later heard that the EPA reported to the command post as if going to take charge and put a stop to this incident. Once they got one look at this holocaust, they backed away like puppies chased by a broom.

Sitting quietly, I was in awe of the powerful presence I had witnessed. I looked into the bright eyes of all the rookies and wondered which ones would be around for the next mammoth conflagration. I was thrilled and proud that we faced down this demon. We definitely played like champions today.

*Our faith on fire determination worked!*

## Boiling Liquid Expanding Vapor Explosion

Firefighters had set ladder pipes all around the burning rail cars. The train was carrying flammable liquids. One firefighter climbed to the top of the ladder to direct the nozzle flow. The loud hissing noise was his first clue of a problem. The second clue came and went in seconds. The whistling sound of the metal vessel rupturing only lasted a few seconds. The explosion blew the ladder, engine and all it contained to smithereens. Parts of the fire engine were found as far away as two miles. The firefighter was never found. He was obliterated into unrecognizable pieces.

I turned off the video and turned to my class of rookies.

"This is the fire we will be fighting tonight," I warned with a serious face.

We went through the coordinated events. We walked in unison while maintaining a team effort when fire is literally in your face. This exercise tests courage and resolve for both the rookies and the instructor.

As the sun began to set on burn night, the rookies lined up on each side of the hose line facing the large propane tank, and I was standing in the middle of them. Nodding, I gave the instructor operating the propane simulator a thumbs-up. The gas roared, and the tank lit up like a massive bonfire. We marched in an arranged fashion toward the fire. We targeted the upper portion (vapor space) of the vessel with hose line. The goal is to cool the product as it boils and turns to a vapor, preventing it from stressing the container and exploding. Thus the boiling liquid expanding vapor explosion referred to as BLEVE.

*Blast leveling everything very effectively—including firefighters.*

As we moved closer to the vessel, we expanded our nozzle to a fog pattern per our training guidelines. The team held tight as we approached the tank, and the flames shrieked from the tank, warning it was about to blow.

BLEVEs are a triple whammy hazard. They have a chemical inside that can hurt you. They have a container that can rupture and hurt you and if flammable can burn you.

Leading the group, I reached with my gloved hand up inside the fire to turn the valve located on top of the five hundred gallon propane container. The fire suddenly flashed in size toward my face, burning my eyebrows and eyelashes. My team wavered gently to one side avoiding the flames, but they held their position. I gave a quick evil eye to the now smirking instructor operating the controls. Again, I reached up inside the fire to turn off the valve and this time the fire went out.

Looking back I saw that the instructor working the control was now laughing. The other instructors witnessing this drama high-fived the instructor operating the controls for his fine job of jacking with my rookies and me.

The instructor waited until I was on top of the propane fire, then he turned the knob to blast.

*Agitator! Another test. I passed, thank God.*

It was a miracle my rookies and I were not severely burned. I was not happy about the loss of my eyebrows and eyelashes, but it is part of the never-ending tradition—agitation. Like a mother hen, I raised hell, squawking at my fellow instructors, but to win at this game was impossible.

My miracle came in taking it on the chin.

Dedication: This story is dedicated to all the rookies that suffer agitation. Keep your chin up and a smile on your face. When you grow up, go easy on the rookies you train.

# 9/11

*Sounds of sirens tend to bother and reassure me simultaneously.*

Our first son Johnathan had been accepted at WestPoint, the country's most prestigious military academy. John would spend one year at the WestPoint prep school and then on to the WestPoint military academy for the next four years, becoming an army officer. This was the beginning of a new chapter in our lives. We were very proud of both our sons Johnathan and Grant. Johnathan was the first to leave the nest.

My husband, Sam, and I booked a special graduation trip. Our plan was to travel to New York and spend a few days sightseeing then at the appointed time, we would happily, but regrettably, hand Johnathan over to the federal government.

On July 11, 2001, we checked in at the World Trade Center Marriott. Over the next few days we went atop the World Trade Center, ate at Windows on the World and picked up the perfect Christmas ornament at the gift shop to commemorate our visit.

On July 14, 2001, we took John to the prep school. We met the teachers, sergeants and then spent the afternoon crying in each other's arms in a motel nestled by the sea. Our first child had now left our nest. John was a good boy—he enriched our lives.

Our last sight of John on that trip was when we returned to Fort Monmouth to watch him in a military parade. He had only been at the prep school for half a day, but with his new buzz haircut, he marched and paraded in unison with the other members.

John smiled with that "Come on mom, do not cry, I am okay," look on his face.

It was now time for us to leave John and return home and open a new chapter, focusing on our second son, Grant who had a great future too.

When leaving the West Point prep school, I cried some more. When boarding the plane, I cried some more. When I got home, I cried even more.

Little did I know that this was the beginning of a tough year, a lot of crying, not only for this mother, but for every American. There were more tears of brokenness to be shed.

Most Americans agree they will never forget where they were, or what they were doing during the 9/11 attacks. While teaching CPR in a construction company in Richardson, Texas, a company supervisor interrupted my class to say that America had been attacked, "A plane had hit the World Trade Center."

*Surely not? He has got to be kidding. Nobody would do that to us would they?*

Shrugging in disbelief, I kept teaching.

The lesson was interrupted again, "Two planes now," the supervisor said, a higher level of panic in his voice. This time people got up and left the room. Class was over.

Living secure in denial, I thought, "No way." But my lunch break was spent sitting at a conference table watching replays on the television as the planes hit the towers over and over.

*Impossible!*

Until now, I had always felt like Teflon. Maybe it was just the confidence of youth. I felt nothing could touch me, and if it did, I believed God would protect me. Now my safety and security was challenged in a new way. This lack of security caused me to begin to question God over and over.

*God, are you there? What is going on? What does all of this mean? God, my boy is up there right next to all this? God! What do I do? Protect him, God.*

The worst possible event an American could imagine, and I watched the best of the NYFD enter the World Trade Center Towers like ants pouring toward a picnic, rolling with gumption, determination and a distilled bravery never seen before in the fire service in America. Then the buildings began to collapse.

Watching with my hands to my head and my eyes widened, my blood pressure rose to a palpable level. A distinct panic, fear, unbelief, and uncertainty enveloped me. My *faith on fire* flickered.

"Command to any unit in *2 World Trade Center*."

Silence. Silence. Silence.

Silence became the sound of death and destruction. The sound of life as we knew it was gone in the blink of an eye.

I wailed with a level of grief I never had before experienced, a guttural sound that came from deep within—a sound of agony, of death and of disbelief. It pierced my heart in such a way that it cannot be adequately described.

*God! No! Please this can't be!*

Brother and sister firefighters, 343 of them, died inside the twin towers. I could not believe what was before my eyes. This was suffering, not just for me, but also for any human being that believed in a better way—a better life—life filled with love and family.

*Did it roar with warning? Did the New York firefighters realize what was happening? Did they have time to make peace with God?*

My son Johnathan called home several times. He could see the smoke from the barracks at the prep school. At first, I could tell something was bothering him, but I did not know what it was, other than the obvious.

Each time he called his voice got stronger and stronger and finally he said, "Mom, I am coming home, I want to be a firefighter-paramedic." I cried some more.

My second son, Grant was also entering a fire explorer program, and I cried some more.

*God! The plan was for my children to have a better life than me—to be an army officer and to get a great education. Not to follow in my footsteps.*

It was one thing for me to be a firefighter, but another to visualize either of my sons humping it up a flight of stairs to a fire like 9/11. Where would I get the faith for this?

My faith was being smothered and fear flooded in my heart.

To put myself, my friends, my co-workers or, God forbid, my child in their place was just too much to imagine.

The New York City police, fire, emergency medical services, port authority and others repeatedly showed the rest of the world what American emergency service workers were made of. I was proud to witness their love and heroic acts. At the same time, I was incredibly torn by their sacrifice. I shudder to think about a brother or sister in our department giving this sacrifice. But I cannot even bring myself to think about my children doing the same.

It is hard to understand why Americans are so hated. Humans are so used to being right and making others wrong. No matter the race, creed, color, religion or sexual orientation, our primary job is to love one another.

*I am guilty make others wrong. I do not show all the love I need to. Oh God! I am so sorry.*

The entire country, as well as most of the world, experienced a degree of post-traumatic stress disorder from September 11.

*Can any good come from these impossibly horrific events?*

People are in this world together, and together we can do anything. Surviving as a nation, a world requires us to keep our integrity and keep our faith. Suffering is one of our greatest teachers in life.

*Pushing through the pain is what separates the winners from the losers.*

The next on duty shift after 9/11, our lieutenant gathered us in the kitchen and asked, "If we faced a 9/11 event today, what would you do? Would you be willing to give your life like the NYFD did?"

Each of us had to evaluate our call and commitment to the job. Did we have the mettle to stand against such a threat? Were we willing to be the first line of defense of our homeland?

When forced to answer that question I said, "Yes!"

*There are those that think they can and there are those that think they can't. They are both right!*

That yes began to rekindle my faith. A challenge by my officer created a new possibility for me. Suddenly, I realized, this horrible event served to refuel my faith. Firefighters know how to face the impossible together.

*We are champions and we play and practice like champions! New York Fire Department is full of champions!*

What could I do to honor those who lay their life on the line?

*I could live a big, bold, life in the face of tragedy! That is what I can do! My life has been awesome! I have lived life on the razors edge of light and darkness. The first ingredient of my miracle really is the impossible!*

Johnathan opted out of West Point early. That broke my heart, but he fulfilled on his promise, came home and is now a fire lieutenant and paramedic in east Texas. The boys at West Point in John's class ended up in Iraq and Afghanistan. What seemed like a bad decision back then, ended up being a good decision, because many of John's friends did not make it out alive. It's possible my son also could not have come home alive. God is so good to deliver unanswered prayers at the right time and at a moment when they are needed. Grant changed his mind and chose a different career path, not as risky as firefighting.

*Thank God! I love my children and want the best for them. They, too, are my miracle.*

This is when I realized the terrorist acts left a hole in my heart that only my faith has been able to fill. The NYFD showed us bravery and love. They suffered the impossible and those of us watching were amazed and honored by their sacrifice. The New York Fire Department showed the world how to lay down your life for others—they paid the ultimate sacrifice.

*The ultimate demonstration of love in action. This is what firefighters, paramedics and police do.*

> "We know what real love is because Jesus gave up his life for us. So we also ought to give up our lives for our brothers and sisters."
> —1 John 3:16, NLT

Dedication: This story is dedicated to all the lives lost due to 9/11. Most people only remember 343 firefighters, but more firefighters have died since 9/11 due to respiratory and cancer complications from the dust. You are not forgotten.

## Arson Goes High Tech

In February of 2008, members of Dallas Fire Department believed an arsonist was born in our city. We were wrong. Quintuple arsonists were born. The fire-setting thrills started small with trashcans and port potties, but soon graduated to bigger items—vehicles. The first weekend of life for these firebugs equaled twelve car fires. The dark births triggered the Dallas Fire Department's arson division into full swing and firefighters spent countless hours risking their lives for the amusement of a few.

Not since the church hate crime fires back in early 1990s has the arson division seen such an in-depth investigation. The discovery started by canvassing the neighborhoods and talking to people about what they had seen or heard. It was determined early on that the fires involved several school-aged males.

On March 8, there were four more fires of the same type and pattern. The hunt for juvenile fire setter's intensified. One early clue in the investigation was a "white SUV and a gold car." The team targeted their surveillance of these vehicles. Dallas Fire Department, as well as police undercover officers, supported heavy surveillance.

Since the baby firebugs chose the cover of darkness in which to operate, the investigators were forced to have a stealth-like presence throughout the city. Arson investigators do not traditionally operate in undercover mode. This team, however worked 24/7 including late night details spent in stakeout vehicles.

"There is nothing worse than being undercover, hunkered down in a vehicle on a dark street and hear gun shots. It was so bad out there, that for a while police were stopping police," said one lead investigator.

As the number of vehicle fires rose, citizens cried out for war on the arsonist. City officials became involved and council persons were demanding swift action.

As the investigation expanded, fire activity suddenly dropped. Frustration grew, but the investigation team held tight. The investigators knew it was only time between this sudden lack of activity and a full arrest.

Thirty-nine days from the start there was noted movement by the suspects. The lead suspect snuck out of his house after the school prom. He was still dressed in a rented tux and patent leather shoes. He made rounds to gather other would-be arsonists. There was a quick stop at a local gas station. They spent $3.30 filling a small gas can. This carload of teens thrived off the smell of gasoline and the explosive power of fuel and match. They were set for a late night of fiery entertainment.

With fuel stored for later use, the conversation was directed at the newest member of the group.

"It's your turn to light the fire," one older teen said to the newest twelve-year-old member.

"No! I am not starting the fire."

"Yes, you have to take Mike's place since he cannot be here," said the older teen.

"No! I will not," he argued.

"Okay, I will start this one, but you're gonna do the next one," the leader said with authority.

The teens cruised several neighborhoods looking for the right spot to strike. They had no idea police helicopter, Air One, was silently tracking them from above. The helicopter documented the night's activities via infrared video. The heat from the car's engine outlined the vehicle.

Two teens got out of their car now located inside Kiest Park. The infrared camera reflected heat from their glow-in-the-dark outlined bodies. One teen poured the gasoline, and the other struck and threw the match onto a portapotty and a small fireball lit up the dark sky.

The leader, still wearing his rented tux and patented leather shoes from the prom, was standing too close to the flames. His shoes caught fire, and he began to stomp his feet. Both assailants got back into the car. The group headed out of the park and onto Highway 67 looking for more destruction. The youngest of the group still had to prove himself worthy.

The car entered another neighborhood. They carefully scrutinized each potential target. The job had to look and feel right. They came to a stop and two firebugs got out of the car with the gas can and approached a new target.

On entering a new neighborhood, the firebugs selected a vehicle to set on fire. Two undercover agents were buried up inside the car now targeted by the youths. The undercover agents held their breath and slowly drew their weapons.

*Impossible!*

A sudden flick of a porch light spooked the two teens and they stopped in their tracks and then ran back to their car. The two undercover police and fire officers released their trapped breath and holstered their guns.

*Just in time miracle!*

The suspects backed up and targeted a different car a few houses up ahead. The same two teens got out, poured the gasoline, struck the match and lit up the sky. They ran back to their car and sped away then soon realized someone was following them. The police/fire command post ordered a unified response that would end in felony arrests of all the youth.

The infrared camera rolling in Air One, showed the police surrounding the boys' vehicle. Once the vehicle stopped, police stood one foot in front of the other, guns drawn. The boys obediently got out of the car, hands in the air, knelt down to the ground, and laid with their faces on the ground. The police clicked the handcuffs in place.

On April 6, 2008, four teenagers were arrested for arson and an array of vandalism and criminal mischief complaints.

Two of the teens refused to talk and two others sang like little mockingbirds. Investigators found out all they needed to know. The little birds even told investigators why the temporary lull in the fire activities. It was caused by the parents of the ringleader grounding him.

*Double miracle!*

Imagine that? Parental supervision prevented arson, at least for a few weeks. Once the grounding was over, the leader was allowed to go to prom, have access to the car and light more fires. The leader of the group was an illegal alien from Mexico. He hated America and school. The motive of this arson was rebellion.

Five teens were charged with arson. The twelve-year-old was released, because he resisted the pressure to light a fire, and he told the truth.

*The truth set him free.*

One of the best miracles in our society is close parenting. Parents do not understand the powerful and positive effect discipline has on their children. I am not talking about spanking. I am talking about being present, talking to and listening to our children. Discipline says, I love you and I care about you to a child. Our entire society operates off of integrity. Integrity is doing what you are supposed to do and honoring your word when no one is looking.

When people talk of miracles, they always think of something supernatural that is not supposed to be. Sometimes a miracle is just having integrity, and it starts at the top of organizations and families.

Dedication: This story is dedicated to all the arson and prevention officers that work behind the scenes to keep people safe.

# Chapter 9

# BACK DRAFT

Definition: A smoke explosion caused by insufficient oxygen to sustain the fire. Rapid introduction of oxygen (improper ventilation) feeds this dangerous link.

## The Last Alarm

Steak and baked potato was on the dinner menu tonight at the station—it was delicious! We sat back with our bellies full and picked our teeth before doing the dishes. After the dishes were done, I made a pot of coffee, and Capt. and I sat talking.

He had taken a few shifts off sick, which was not like him, and I asked him point blank, "What's wrong?"

Capt. always looked you straight in the eye when talking to you. He talked directly at you and made each person feel special that way. He listened this way too, never interrupting. He was a gentle spirit who was loved by everyone.

Knowing he had a heart attack several years ago, I handed him a cup of black coffee and asked, "Why have you been off sick?"

He looked at me and said, "I have been having some chest pains."

Glaring back at him with not only a paramedic eye but also that of an American Heart Association emergency cardiac care educator, I frowned.

*What is he telling me?*

"Is it serious, Capt.? What did the doctor say?"

"I did not go to the doctor," he said flatly.

*He had already made his decision—impossible! He is in denial, a psychological sign of heart attack.*

Swallowing hard, I bit my tongue, exhaling in frustration. I was going to let this simmer in my dark room, but the bell hit—we had a structure fire.

The fire was only a few blocks from the station. Engine 56 reported out with a lot of fire on second floor of a two-story house. I set up the command post and transmitted two alarms on the fire. It looked as though the firefighters were doing a good job of heading off the fire, with white steam coming off the roof. Suddenly, the white steam turned back to a heavy black smoke, and the fire grew.

*Dang it! It is getting away from them.*

Out of the corner of my eye, firefighters carried a body out of the house. Once on the ground, they feverishly pumped the chest of their patient—CPR.

*A fire fatality!*

The driver-engineer came by and I said, "I need information on the citizen they're doing CPR on, I have to make a report to arson."

"It is not a citizen they are doing CPR on, it's Capt."

"What?" I asked, but I already knew.

With titanic tears in his ice blue eyes, the driver-engineer said, "They were on the second floor getting after the fire and Capt. fell forward, flat on his face. They thought he had just tripped at first, but then he would not move, so they dropped the hose lines and drug him out. No pulse—CPR." He dropped his head and walked off to help direct the paramedics onto the scene.

*Impossible!*

Other apparatus showed up to help us with the fire and eventually the fire went out, but a bigger fire was stoked in our hearts. We passed command to other arriving companies and headed to the hospital hoping for the best.

Hundreds of firefighters and police officers lined the doors at Medical City Hospital located on Forest Lane in North Dallas. Hospital personnel cut us a lot of slack when a brother/sister dies. We hover for hours, we stand guard, we protect the body, we do any and everything possible that we can. We entered where Capt. laid motionless and gradually turning an ashy greyish-blue.

*No, God! This is one of the good ones! No, we need to keep him on this earth. Give him back God!*

We stood defiantly asking God why? Some cried silently. There was no calm for the fear or confusion running amuck in our minds. We were expecting a miracle for Capt., his family and all of us. Instead we all choked down reality.

Having dealt with the agitation and harassment in the department was a piece of cake, but I could not deal with this. Grief filled tears poured from my eyes and down my cheeks. I was stunned.

*God, where are you?*

Others stood challenging God one moment, dropping their heads in defeat the next. Some looked up and away as if still bargaining with God.

Capt.'s wife showed up at the hospital, she was a precious, gentle woman. Capt. always talked joyfully about her. She was his rock. She stood taller than him, and he had always looked at her proudly and his eyes dilated—a look of love. Capt.'s thoughts, ideas and focus were family—his primary concern. Capt. was an example to all on loving one's family and loving all of us. Our hearts broke open while thoughts of how his family would survive quaked in our thoughts.

Amazingly, Capt.'s wife loved us during this time. She had every right to be concerned with herself and her family, but she was also concerned with us. She was a loving person just like Capt. had said.

The chief and I were ordered back to the station—we now had mountains of paperwork and reports to do. Line-of-duty-death reports are unending. What was the number of runs made this shifts? What kind of emergency runs did we make? What did we eat during the shift? When was his last medical physical? Were there any visitors to the station? You name it they asked it. Chief and I stayed up all night preparing reports. The engine crew left and headed to Capt.'s house to support his wife. Our station was placed out of service for the rest of the shift. The chief and I *gutted it up* all night long, with heavy hearts, while wiping tears of frustration from our exhausted eyes.

*This is no way to grieve.*

The chaplains of the Dallas Fire Department planned the funeral. It was a huge event. Chief and I buffed our shoes, checked that our insignias were pinned correctly, double checked that our shirts were tucked in smoothly and put our uniform hat under our right arm when not on our head. Walking out the door, we striped our badges with black tape as a sign of mourning. Flags flew at half-staff across the city. The smell of sorrow filled the air.

Not only do firefighters work together, we live together, we share everything a family shares including the death of one of our own. Capt. was one of our own.

When there is a line-of-duty-death (LODD), travelers come from every corner of the nation. There were also uniformed officers from across the State of Texas at the funeral. Unity, solidarity and brotHERhood are cemented together during a LODD.

Chief and I sat among the crowd feeling like two dots in a sea of blue uniforms. Flags flew, bag pipes played, and drums beat. Capt.'s casket was carried on the engine he rode to his last alarm; Engine 56 was draped in black.

At the cemetery, uniformed officers held their rifles to their shoulders and with precision and sequence, fired twenty-one times. The chaplain said the final goodbye to a brother, friend and true leader.

Capt. was the quintessential firefighter's officer. He was smart, kind, and an honorable man. He treated people with respect and appreciated the uniqueness that *all* members brought to his team. I attended Capt.'s wedding and now had attended his funeral.

Capt. was a miracle to me. When Capt. was a lieutenant, I had suffered with the supervisor in recruiting and shortly after, I was assigned to work under him. He had breathed life back into me. He was supportive, gave guidance and shared his joy. When the Bubba Club reared their ugly heads, Capt. stood up and said what needed to be said. He was present and as an officer, you could count on him as a friend. Capt. loved us all—he even loved the scally wags. He expected the best from everyone.

*Thank you, God, for this man. He was an awesome man. He showed me kindness when I needed it most. When I was facing the impossible, Capt. was my miracle.*

The death of Capt. began a downward spiral for me. It was a difficult time to say the least. There is no course on how to feel, act or be in death, especially when you lose a brother and a true friend. It is still difficult to talk about it.

Decades of harassment, agitation, frustration and aggravation mounted on top of Capt.'s death resulted in an internal inferno in my heart. Add the events of 9/11, and I was ready for an emotional back draft. I was a seven-alarm fire. I did not conquer it on my own. God, like a penciling technique in a flashover cooled my flames even though I was the one to strike the match and light the fire.

*How do I push past this pain, God?*

Not long after Capt. died, our deputy chief called Battalion 2 to his office. This deputy's behavior and attitude toward people defined the very word *egotistical*, and he had snapped at me on the phone when I tried to clarify my understanding of something. Since I was part of his team, I requested he show me the respect of a team member when talking to me. In addition, a few weeks prior I had heard him speak disrespectfully to his wife on the phone when in his office. I didn't like it and somebody needed to teach him a lesson. I nominated myself.

The deputy didn't want to show mutual respect to others and in a commanding tone snapped at me again. I responded with "Yes sir," and then put my request in writing. The next shift, the deputy asked me to call him on a private line. He had obviously given my request much more meaning than necessary. He didn't like it when a woman spoke clearly and plainly, holding firm in requesting mutual respect as a team member. This little private phone call was a prelude of what was to come and determined, I made my request for mutual respect again.

*He cannot be allowed to get comfortable disrespecting me or any other woman.*

Shortly thereafter, my battalion chief and I were called to the deputy chief's office for a meeting. The good news is, I was not alone and together we would serve as a kicking post for the deputy.

*My request for mutual respect got him out of his glossy little shell and dug under his skin.*

We reported to the deputy's office on schedule. Immediately, I could tell he was about to peel off some of our backside and hand it back to us—like a cold, steel, gurney in the morgue.

Sensing his ruthlessness side, I tried to get comfortable in his presence—a man who was literally the most inauthentic person I had ever known, next to the Duke. He looked back at me with the same respect he would give a cockroach. My eyes opened to slits.

The deputy turned to us and snarled, "What I am about to tell you, you will not respond to. Then you will get up and leave without having said a word. Have I made myself clear?"

*Nothing like a one-sided conversation. Why not just talk to yourself!*

He twisted his lips into a sardonic smile and looked down on me like a hawk about to swoop down on a mouse. The deputy was about to take a rifle approach—not a shotgun. It was clear he wanted a direct hit that would cause cavitation in my heart and soul. We had our marching orders to be good little followers, not to think, or say anything. I could not keep up a believable pretense and eyed him with the passion of a zombie.

This deputy chief and I went way back. I knew him when he was a lieutenant. He was good at firefighting, but horrible at handling people. He often talked down to others and kicked them while they were down. He presented his agitation as playful in the past. Today with the stars on his collar, the agitation had now turned to abuse of his authority—at least this was my belief.

The deputy aimed his comments to me derisively. "You will not put anything in writing without my prior approval!" The smell of annoyance was in the air.

*I guess my attention to detail in how he communicates with women is too meticulous for him.*

He turned toward my chief; it was his turn for a verbal whipping. "If you want to ride out this job until retirement, you will do as I say!" He said it much calmer than the lightning storm inside my brain.

*Threatening the old man and his retirement? Geez what leadership!*

The deputy was so rude and unkind to my battalion chief, it made me sick. He had beaten him down to a mushroom head. In a moment of pristine clarity, I knew the fight was on.

*You can say anything to me you want to, but you cannot talk to my chief that way. He is ten times the leader you are!*

I did not know if I was furious because I could not do anything about what was happening or about not being able to say a word.

*Not able to say a word!*

Today, the deputy won, but he had now declared war and poured gasoline on an already hot fire. We would come into each other's circle again. I was going to make sure he got a taste of *who* he was—for me and for my chief. Although I did not know it at the time, it would be for many other Bubbas too. We got up to leave and did not say goodbye. That will teach him! I thought in a silent scream.

*He thinks he is at the core of the world with no concern for others!*

The deputy liked to talk and throw his power and authority around. He really did not understand that we were all watching him intently.

*Watching. Listening. Sharing. Writing it all down.*

Little did I know that I was about to supply the dangerous link to volatile fuel and cause a back draft in relationships that I could never again repair.

## Resigned and Cynical

Walking away from the harsh and fuming deputy's office that day, I was resigned and cynical about the Dallas Fire Department and its leadership. For twenty-five years I have loved the department, tolerated the agitation and forgave. Now my heart was full of a raging fire ready to flash.

*I have to be a team player. I showed respect for him when sharing my frustration over his disrespect toward me. I have had to take whatever came my way on the chin. Even agitation! Agitation? Hmm . . . Maybe that is what the deputy needs, a little agitation! It sure humbled me many times over.*

I had been tied up, man-handled and put in a mop sink, and written about in other poop sheets—all pretty harmless and sometimes funny agitation. The ultimate in fire station agitation that delivered the biggest punch was the written underground grapevine.

*"You will not put anything in writing without my prior approval!" Hmm . . . Words will be my kindling, and I am about to build a bonfire. The deputies own inflated ego will serve as the fuel. This will be as easy as taking candy from a baby. The deputy's reaction alone will create high level entertainment.*

There were poop sheets about my knee injuries, telephone calls and other assorted adventures. Some poop sheets were nothing but awards. They were not Academy Awards, but I found some of them hilariously funny.

After all, Ferrelli told me, "If they like you, they will agitate you. If they do not like you, they will not even talk to you."

*I think I like the deputy! He is a chest beater where woman are concerned, but I like him because he is pure entertainment! He obviously needs some special attention.*

When I left Station 3 due to a promotion, I agitated some of the guys, and it was a hilarious day with lots of laughter. I brought in steaks to celebrate and gave out awards to all my Bubba friends. I gave a pacifier to one guy for being a crybaby. Another I gave hemorrhoid cream, and I will leave to your imagination as to why? The firefighters receiving these awards accepted them with a smile. Some of the awards I received during my career are not appropriate for conversation, but I took it on the chin—smiling and maintaining my joy.

*This deputy is an over-gown wimp and needs a little agitation to break his conceited spirit.*

Agitation was meant to keep me grounded and test my resolve to hang on in the face of difficult and disappointing reports. I laughed off every event—which is exactly what this deputy dog should have done, but he was not that clever—I knew it. Thinking about seeing the deputy's face and big schnozzle turning blood red—I smiled devilishly.

The seed of my writing was planted while at Station 3 where most of the poop sheets were written about me. A previous mayor was a writer for the *Dallas Observer*, a local newspaper, and she knocked many of her stories out of the proverbial park with her caustic honesty—she was a great teacher.

While at Station 2, I tested my writing skills with my newsletter called the *Fire Rescue Poop Sheet*. I wrote "Body by Bluebell," about the effects on our mule belly when eating ice cream every shift. "Neuro-linguistics of Miss-Communication" covered our inability to recognize each team member's primary communication language as well as other assorted misadventures. It was lighthearted fun and took the edge off some difficult situations involving the Bubbas' personalities. Poop sheets usually resulted in lots of laughter and entertainment, at least this was the expectation of the Bubbas when they were about me. The Dallas Fire Departments rules and regulations supported the precious tradition of agitation.

*Agitation was acceptable when pushed down on the lower ranks. How is it going to look when the agitation is pushed up on ranking individuals? They allow these rules so let's see how they like them?*

Having to sit quietly and listen to the pompous deputy chief, I knew I would become a liability for my battalion chief. I made the decision to transfer. I called another deputy chief in communications and offered to work for him, and he immediately requested me; I did not even have to fill out a transfer request. Once I was free of the deputy dog's command, the fun began.

*Patience is all I need now! Timing is everything.*

Several firefighters told me a story about the deputy chief's behavior while at a conference in Houston when he was representing the Dallas Fire Department. It was reported that at various points the deputy had appeared drunk, badgered the hotel staff, belittled a waitress and talked about doing some other not-so-appropriate things in his above normal, irritating voice.

Dallas Fire Department personnel were reported to be "startled, mortified and embarrassed by his remarks," as one firefighter put it.

Despite his behavior, this deputy dog received no formal punishment from the department for his actions while in Houston.

The department had an unwritten rule, "Protect ranking individuals at any cost, especially at deputy level or higher." This rule appeared to be alive and well.

Stories reported to me were proven true and people were in agreement. Facts were checked and double-checked, and it all pointed toward self-destructive behavior by the deputy. It became clear the department held rank-in-file members to a higher standard, yet handled the upper echelon with kid gloves. Maybe a stern warning would go out to the deputy chiefs, but paperwork-wise, the slate was squeaky clean.

*Something has to be done! Never trust your tongue or pen when your heart is bitter.*

There was something I was missing for sure—tact. I read somewhere that tact was building a fire under people without making their blood boil. I was about to make the deputy's blood boil over and he was already a hot head.

*Deputy dog needs a dose of the Fire Rescue Poop Sheet!*

This was the perfect opportunity for the *Fire Rescue Poop Sheet* to rise again. The deputy chief was the perfect target. It would be easy to find words loaded with dynamite where he is concerned.

This was not my proudest moment, but there was something I needed to learn. Sometimes it just has to be the hard way.

"This entire Poop Sheet is dedicated to a certain deputy chief who is such an awesome example to all the subordinates in the field. The Fire Rescue Poop Sheet is back by popular demand. More issues are planned in the future. Remember, any day, any time the Poop Sheet author could be watching. Enjoy!"

### POEM—I AM A DEPUTY

I am chief, guess who I am; I keep my head deep in the sand.

I drink too much and cheat and steal,

I make extra money off free buffet meals.

I do not understand the word integrity;

I believe I was raised great, with superiority.

My belly is big and so is my head,

to listen to me talk makes one wish he were dead,

. . . But I do not see a bad side of me,

I'm perfect, I'm chief, I'm a deputy. . . .

Guilty of a tasteless attempt to slam another human being, my faith flame flickered like a candle in a windstorm. Deep down inside, I knew I hurt when it was done to me, and still I turned off love and allowed negativity to sink deeper into my heart.

However, I did meet with the approval of most of the Bubbas. I justified this kind of agitation at the time as it fit into our subculture—it was tradition. The deputy may have had it coming, but it was not my place to take vengeance; for this I am not proud. What made me think it was right to bring down judgment?

The first few poop sheets were anonymous out of fear of retaliation. I never used the deputy's name either because in all fairness his name was not the issue, it was the behaviors. I just did a good job of describing him. The more I wrote, the bolder I became. I began to put my name on the newsletter and even drummed up advertising.

*Look who has the ego now? I wish I had bottled and sold some of this energy I was wasting—now I am the Bubba Club.*

The deputy chief of fire dispatch, who I consider to be a friend, called me into his office.

"Sherrie, the deputy chief wants you to stop writing about him in the *Fire Rescue Poop Sheet*." My chief appeared embarrassed to have to make the request.

"What makes him think the poop sheet is about him?"

*I never named anyone! Hmm . . . The truth must hit home. My dad would say, "A fox always smells his own home."*

"Not sure how he knows it is about him, but he has asked me to advise you that he will sue you if you do not stop writing about him," my friend shared.

*Sue me? Really, for what will he sue me? The deputy wants to do to me what a drummer does to his drum sets.*

"I do not know, but that is what he asked me to say to you."

"The department investigated [the deputy chief] and corroborated many of Wilson's most damaging accusations. Although the final report on the deputy chief officially did not sustain the accusation that [the deputy chief] was intoxicated while at a conference in Houston, three eyewitnesses more or less portrayed the deputy chief as the second coming of Keith Moon. '[He] appeared intoxicated and consumed between [six] and ten alcoholic beverages in an evening.'"

—Dallas Observer

It was a step in the right direction that the deputy chief was now under investigation. But I had to file the complaint because no one at the top would initiate an investigation against him.

*Impossible! Where is our department's integrity?*

Another Fire Rescue Poop Sheet responded to the deputy chief's whine:

> "Boo, hoo! Boo, hoo! I'm gonna sue. Dish it out but cannot take it, we all know you know who! Now deputy, we haven't told anyone who you are. We have only told the stories (facts) that have been told to us. You're the one doing the talking and drawing attention to yourself..."

The deputy chief kept talking like an out-of-control-maniac. The Bubbas kept telling me what he was saying, and I kept writing it all down.

*The deputy is beating his chest like an animal in the wild. Maybe he would like a new name Tarzan? Me Tarzan, king of the fire department jungle, you lowly woman!*

It was like all the agitation over years began to rise up and venom poured out of my heart. Writing became cathartic and the more I wrote, the more empowered I felt.

In April, the deputy chief filed a lawsuit alleging that the revelations published by the poop sheet caused him "Shame, embarrassment, humiliation, pain and mental anguish."

*Imagine that? He's actually ashamed? Really? Not sure I believe this.*

> "For his assorted misadventures the fifty-three-year-old [deputy chief] received no formal punishment from the department other than a letter of counseling which is basically a mild warning. Now, however, he is suing the female who exposed his frat-boy behavior in a gossipy fire hall newsletter called the Fire Rescue Poop Sheet."
>
> —Dallas Observer

Feeling justified and right this time, I did not even recognize those were the components of my own self-righteousness.

Once the rank-in-file (Bubbas) heard of the lawsuit, they started coming to my aid. Not only did they say they would defend me, they started feeding me more and more stories on the deputy.

*Now I am finally part of the brotHERhood—it is really a Bubba Club.*

Feeling accepted and appreciated for standing up to what I saw was a black eye in the department, I was torn. Had the deputy just learned who he was being for others and kept his mouth shut, it would have all gone away and the media would have not known anything.

*He just keeps beating his chest!*

This mess was an embarrassment to the members of the department, but since leadership would not step up and lead, the Bubbas and I did—with our stories.

The January 2005 issue of the *Fire Rescue Poop Sheet* answered the question, "Why Poop?" We had heard that the higher-ups did not appreciate our newsletter. The firefighters reportedly loved it, but it was not just about entertainment. The poop sheet simply sent home an old message—leadership was non-existent.

What we learned from these stories is that power and influence may come and go, but our actions are connected to our moral values. The values at the Dallas Fire Department had been acquired through tradition and dedicated to service and started with integrity, but firefighters reported sitting around the fire station listening to this elitist brag about how deceitful he was.

The Dallas Fire Department's general philosophy says:

"The honesty and integrity of all members of the department are of vital importance. Not only because of the close working and social relationship, but because of our citizens need for trustworthy city employees. Honesty, veracity, truthfulness and integrity are prerequisites to maintain public confidence."

—DFD Manual of Procedures

Our citizens had grounds to question our department's integrity and our leadership did nothing about it. After filing a complaint against the deputy, I reported to Internal Affairs to defend myself. I claimed my First Amendment rights as a reporter for the *Fire Rescue Poop Sheet* that I had now copyrighted.

The Constitution of the United States protects the right to freedom of religion and freedom of expression from government interference. Freedom of expression consists of the rights to freedom of speech, press, assembly and to petition the government for a redress of grievances, and the implied rights of association and belief. The Supreme Court interprets the extent of the protection afforded to these rights.

The department had never had a situation like this one before! It was as if they were frozen. They would not punish the deputy chief because he was one of them, and there was not much to punish me over.

They allowed the deputy chief to continue with his lawsuit even when I claimed it was because of my whistle-blowing on his loose cannon behavior. Basically, the department did nothing. They were more interested in important things like changing the name of the department from Dallas Fire Department to Dallas Fire Rescue Department.

*Geez! How about focusing on some of the more important things going on around here like the continued harassment of a woman firefighter.*

It was disappointing that the department failed to punish the deputy chief. One media source said it perfectly, "The department doesn't exactly defend how it handled the deputy chief's behavioral lapses."

The incoming chief of the department blamed the previous administration and took no action either.

*Why is it we have no leadership?*

My hand was slapped for using a department fax to distribute a newsletter because I faxed it to my previous battalion chief when he called and requested it. The deputy chief was protected for being a near total failure as a leader in an otherwise good department, but the lawsuit against me continued.

A judge denied the deputy chief's motion to have me reveal my sources so he could sue others too.

*Tarzan is one bitter, I got to have it my way man. He was now after not only me but the Bubbas too.*

The judge ruled that as the publisher of the *Fire Rescue Poop Sheet*, I was entitled to the same legal protection as a working journalist. I held fast and honored my word not to reveal names.

In the April, 2005, edition of the *Fire Rescue Poop Sheet*, I wrote about the deputy chief's bragging to the men at the station again about more inappropriate behavior toward me. Behavior I cannot even describe in detail it is so vulgar and repulsive. Irritated with his continued chest beating, I continued to badger the deputy with entertaining examples of his own behavior. The deputy chief acted like a bull seeing red. He snorted, kicked, horned and bragged some more.

June 12, 2006 the big, pompous deputy chief actually showed up for court. He was wearing a suit, tie, colored-hair, penny loafers and a belly than hung over his belt. He reminded me of the Duke. He pranced in like a ridiculous peacock strutting with feathers fanned out gloriously—like it was all over and he had already won. At first, his appearance was that of a calm, cool idiot who walked with the strange uprightness only found in a guy with hatred in his eyes.

*Sadly, I am just as ugly, if not uglier, for my part in this fiasco.*

The deputy dog's attorney argued that he is not a public official, then agreed in all probability he is a public official. He argued as to whether the publisher is media and then seemed to relent there too. He argued that the *Fire Rescue Poop Sheet* showed malice in our stories.

*Malice?*

We just told what we heard from others who had now signed sworn affidavits stating stories as fact.

*The brotHERhood is backing me up! Wow!*

The deputy's attorney whined, "Her stories are based on rumor, your Honor."

The judge responded, "She has witnesses that say they heard your client say [these things]." The judge appeared exasperated.

The deputy's attorney said, "And he's trying to show he's got malice."

The judge retorted, "He's going to try and show it by saying even though I'll admit that I said something like that joking around, it isn't true. The fact that it is not true, which I'm going to try to show at trial, indicates malice?"

The judge, seeming frustrated, wiped his brow, rubbed his neck and finally, held up his palms and said, "I need to know how that works because I do not understand that it (the law) functions that way." I watched as the deputy's face turned a hot-headed red, as his attorney was losing and badly.

*Say "Uncle," Tarzan!*

The deputy's attorney whined, "Judge, she twisted the facts and malice is an issue to be determined at trial."

The judge responded, "You do not have to have any facts for trial? Where is it she twisted the facts? Her evidence corroborates her stories. She has affidavits signed by members that support her stories. These members say the deputy said those things. As a judge, I am a public figure, and I must guard what I say. A deputy chief is a public figure, and he should guard what he says."

The judge went on to say, "Which statement is it the deputy makes that she (the publisher) is entitled to believe? Should she believe the statements he made at the fire station, or the ones he is making now?"

The judge dismissed the case.

## The Price of Integrity

The next *Fire Rescue Poop Sheet* published, started like this:
Cost of parking at court two days. $14.00
Cost of mediation that did not work. $450.00
Cost of legal defense: $12,000.00 to $15,000.00
Winning afrivolous lawsuit . . . PRICELESS!

Fire Rescue Poop Sheet Is Baaaaack! Our vacation stemmed from a frivolous lawsuit brought by a deputy chief. We won the case on motion for summary judgment.

*Winning turned out to be about a twenty-thousand dollar lesson.*

## Fire Rescue Poop Newsletter
### "Our Views, Our Voice"
firerescuepoop@yahoo.com

*Cost of parking at court two days $14.00*
*Cost of mediation that didn't work $450.00*
*Cost of legal defense $12,000.00 to $15,000.00*

June 2006
© Copyright 2006
S.C. Wilson, Publisher
PO BOX 740273
Dallas, Texas 75374

### Winning A Frivolous Lawsuit...PRICELESS!

The Fire Rescue Poop Sheet is back! Our vacation stemmed from a frivolous lawsuit bought by a Deputy Chief. We won the case on motion for summary judgment. The judge determined that the case did not have the merit to go to trial.

The judge clearly understood what was going on and quoted (in detail) affidavits made by members of the Fire Rescue Department. The judge said, "she (the publisher) is a journalist and he (the deputy) is a public figure. What the deputy whispered in the back room, the publisher shouted from the housetops. This is completely legal."

The deputy's attorney responded, "judge, she twisted the facts and malice is an issue to be determined at trial."

The judge responded, "You don't have to have any facts for trial? Where is it she twisted the facts? Her evidence corroborates her stories. She has affidavits signed by members that support her stories. These members say the deputy said those things. As a judge, I am a public figure and I must guard what I say. A Deputy Chief is also a public figure and he should guard what he says." The judge used the example, "You can't hold the Dallas Morning News responsible for reporting what the mayor said, even if he wants to change her story."   Continued page 3

### Rethinking Our Subculture

The short story, *The Lottery*, tells of a community preparing for an upcoming raffle. Excitement grows in the community as people speculate on who is going to win. Names are carefully placed in a wooden box while the children are playing and gathering small stones down by the river. As the town comes together, families hold hands while praying, hoping and wishing for the best. As the annual tradition comes to a climax, one person is selected as the winner. A hush goes out over the crowd as the name is drawn and announced.

Everyone then turns towards the wide-eyed and anxious winner now nervously backing away from its very own close knit society. In a matter of minutes the normally quiet, loving and easy-going crowd of people turn and the chosen sacrifice is then stoned to death. This is an extreme example of tradition gone awry. It leaves this society struggling with its past choices and customs, in addition to the cost and what payoff.   Continued on page 2

### Warmhearted Consideration

We all percolated while waiting, then the buses arrived and we sprang to life. The firefighters association hosted members of the State School at Six Flags for the fortieth year. I did something I haven't done in a while, I volunteered to help. Actually, I was feeling guilty because, I overheard someone say that only twenty-six firefighters had signed up. Reportedly, we needed a hundred, thus my guilt, followed by my action.   Continued page 2

### IN THIS ISSUE
1. Winning Priceless...
2. Rethinking Our...
3. Warmhearted...
4. Welcome Chief

### Disclaimer

To the best of our knowledge, these stories, descriptions, quotes and secrets told inside the *FRP* newsletter are based on fact. The names of individuals actually involved in the stories have been changed, or intentionally left out in order to protect those who may be guilty and/or innocent.

The Publisher

### Request

Members of the Firefighters Association are considering helping publisher Sherrie Wilson with some of the cost of the lawsuit. We feel the positive outcome of this lawsuit has a benefit to every member. A motion has been made to donate five thousand dollars. The motion was delayed pending a ruling from IAFF, since both parties are members. This support will be voted on at the June meetings. Your vote in favor of the original motion will be appreciated. Whatever happens, I want to thank everyone who has been supportive during the lawsuit. I have found your positive support overwhelming.

Sherrie C. Wilson
Publisher

Fire Rescue Poop Newsletter

"Adding to [The deputy chief's] induced misery, Wilson has resumed publication of the *Fire Rescue Poop Sheet,* which was effectively suspended during the lawsuit. Her page-one, above-the-fold headline? 'Winning a Frivolous Lawsuit: Priceless.' We contacted the [deputy chief] himself, and rather than threatening a swift kick [as he had to Wilson], he said only, 'I have no comment for you' before hanging up."

—Dallas Observer

The judge determined that the case did not have the merit to go to trial. "What the deputy whispered in the back room, the publisher shouted from the housetops. This is completely legal."

The good news out of this lawsuit is that we proved that freedom of speech prevails. We can all feel free to speak our minds and state the truth in the future. Management must know that we are watching and expect integrity in their dealing with us.

"In the last scene of the movie, *Saving Private Ryan*, Tom Hanks' character whispers into the ear of Matt Damon's character: "Earn this." True leadership is an earned privilege in any organization, or among members of a team. Just because someone is given a title doesn't mean he/she is a leader."

—Firehouse.com

So yes, justice did its job and had the last word, but I had acted out in frustration and grief. I am clear this was not honorable to the fire service or God.

*I proved I was a hard head and unforgiving. I am the president of my own Bubba Club.*

The firestorm of circumstance was overwhelming me to the point of overtaking and consuming my individual flame of faith. Taking matters into my own hands is not born from faith. In fact, it is just the opposite. My back draft backfired and blew dangerously close to blowing out my faith. I had certainly created another ruckus.

Learning over the years that hurt people, hurt other people, I realized that my pain from previous events in the fire department had to be broken. The shame is that I had a good personality to lead and motivate others, but leadership must be positive to be effective. Kindness trumps ugly perfectionism and being right. I had not been kind to the deputy. When you are so right that you make others wrong, it is an obnoxious right. I learned I do not want to be this kind of right in life. I had to find a way to forgive the deputy for his unkindness to me and my battalion chief. I need to learn to use love as my weapon moving forward.

*God, forgive me. Help me not to be like the deputy.*

No one in history has ever choked to death from swallowing their pride. Deputy forgive me, I was wrong to pick on you. Never again will I be sucked down this negative path.

Dedication: This story is dedicated to the men and women who came to my defense and supported me.

### Facing the Fire
Fire is the good and the bad, the warmth and the pain.
Fire is the light and the dark, the smoke and the flame.
Fire is the day and the night, the loose and the tight.
Fire is the brilliant and beautiful, with colors so bright.
Fire is the curious and devious, the yin and yang.
Facing the fire, facing life, they both are the same.
Sherrie C. Wilson

# Chapter 10

# REFINED BY FIRE

## Love Lesson

"Darkness cannot drive out darkness: only light can do that. Hate cannot drive out hate: only love can do that . . ."

—Martin Luther King, Jr.

Early on in my life I realized that rescuers are unique in that they already possess a deeper love inside their heart for their fellow man. It is why I wanted to be a rescuer. I wanted to help that man at the age of eight, and I wanted to help others. Rescuers die for citizens, proved by 9/11. We die for one another, but in the meantime, we rip each other apart with negative psychosocial games that are lovingly called tradition while failing to live inside team dynamics showing mutual respect.

*God I am so guilty!*

"Love is patient and kind; love does not envy or boast; it is not arrogant or rude. It does not insist on its own way; it is not irritable or resentful; it does not rejoice at wrongdoing, but rejoices with the truth. Love bears all things, believes all things, hopes all things, endures all things."

—1 Corinthians 13:4–7, ESV

Putting people in what we believe is their rightful place is not love. The highest and most positive emotion is love.

*God, I love my friends and family at Dallas Fire Rescue Department. Even that scallywag deputy.*

Following these traditions, I realized how self-righteous my thinking had become. I could not forgive and let go of my own wounds and disappointments, yet I have been forgiven many times when I needed it. Love is one of the strongest emotions and it tends to engulf the person experiencing it. The same could be said about hate.

> "When the Japanese mend broken objects, they aggrandize the damage by filling the cracks with gold. They believe that when something's suffered damage and has a history it becomes more beautiful."
>
> —Billie Mobayed

Thinking back, there had been a time where my charming husband, Sam, loved me through many difficult times—this love meant the world to me. It changed me. The love and forgiveness shown to me transformed me on the inside. Because of Sam loving me through these trials, I became a more loving and dedicated wife to him than I had ever been before.

> "A wise physician said the best medicine for humans is love. Someone then asked, 'What if it doesn't work?' He smiled and answered. 'Increase the dose.'"
>
> —Unknown

Sam had increased the dose of love with me. He taught me an awesome life lesson. I knew in my heart it was time to do the same with the supervisor in recruiting, the deputy dog and those I refer to as the Bubba Club—I had to forgive. When you endeavor to change, you must do so in the spirit of celebration.

*God, is this kind of love an impossible situation for me?*

The path to health and happiness is often not a path of getting your way, but of letting go of your own way. The sad thing is I already knew this. I knew this from deep down within my core, yet I had clung to my defensive posture. The lesson also involved clothing myself in compassion, kindness, humility, gentleness and patience.

*Was my biggest sin lacking love?*

"So now faith, hope, and love abide, these three; but the greatest of these is love."

—1 Corinthians 13:13, ESV

Love binds people together in unity. The only thing that counts is faith expressing itself as love.

## Powerful Words and Conversations

Some science says that we have sixty thousand conversations with ourselves a day. If this is true, nearly every waking moment is full of endless streams of talking with ourselves. If you just argued with this point in your mind, you just had one of those conversations.

When soliloquizing, (talking to ourselves), we generally debate issues back and forth, choose the best action to take, draw conclusions and sometimes choose to jump to them.

When reading that old Cherokee legend, "The Wolves Within," I realized there was a fight going on inside of me and I was not alone. We all have this fight going on in our lives.

An old Cherokee is teaching his grandson about life. "A fight is going on inside me," he said to his grandson. "It's a terrible fight and it is between two wolves. One is evil. He is full of anger, envy, sorrow, regret, greed, arrogance, self-pity, guilt, resentment, inferiority, lies, false pride, superiority, and ego." He continued, "The other is good. He is full of joy, peace, love, hope, serenity, humility, kindness, benevolence, empathy, generosity, truth, compassion, and faith. The same fight is going on inside you. It's inside every person, too."

The grandson thought about it for a minute and then asked his grandfather, "Which wolf wins?"

The old Cherokee smiled knowing the lesson was coming and simply replied, "The one you feed."

Realizing that I chose to feed the bad wolf with the deputy, I needed to create a new possibility in my life and my way of thinking. Recognizing the negative is at play in your life requires self-awareness. Once you are aware of the negative, you must disrupt it and replace it with positive. Our fast-paced, multi-tasking, and plate-spinning lives tend to make us unaware of what is really going on inside of us. Sometimes we just have to slow down and listen to what is inside.

> Our deepest fear is not that we are inadequate. Our deepest fear is that we are powerful beyond measure. It is our light, not our darkness that most frightens us. We ask ourselves, who am I to be brilliant, gorgeous, talented, and fabulous? Actually, who are you not to be? You are a child of God. You're playing small does not serve the world. There is nothing enlightened about shrinking so that other people won't feel insecure around you. We are all meant to shine, as children do. We were born to make manifest the glory of God that is within us. It's not just in some of us; it's in everyone. And as we let our own light shine, we unconsciously give others people permission to do the same. As we are liberated from our own fear, our presence automatically liberates others.
>
> —Marianne Williamson, *A Return to Love*

When back at Station 3 exhausted from run, after run, after run we were manifesting the glory of God within us. We were living powerfully. Somewhere along the way, I lost this powerful, loving, *faith on fire,* winning attitude and way of being. I could blame it on many incidents, but the truth is toughness of mind, not making events mean so much was instilled in me at Station 3.

Words are powerful. We create our world good or bad with our words. Our words become self-fulfilling prophecies.

*Life and death really are in the power of my words and thoughts.*

Having allowed the negative thoughts to seep in, I then put them into action through my words and my accomplishments followed suit. The outcomes were impossible.

We might see "personal fires" along the lines of emotional upsets or other societal problems, and these can include issues in any type of organization. These types of fires have plenty of chain reactions going on. Cooling agents come in the form of cool heads, mutual respect and a loving and related attitude. Rapid cooling comes with the practice of immediate forgiveness. Science now shows that being the cool head in a hot situation is proven to protect your own body functions from ailments such as heart attacks and strokes.

So, how can we make positive deposits when faced with a landslide of daily negative withdrawals? I had to become a student of positive. Reading books, listening to tapes and positive programs helps. Although I struggled staying positive, I have always picked myself up, dusted myself off, and tried again. My miracle was in never giving up on the brotHERhood and never giving up on myself.

If you look at Christ, he created miracles with his words. He calmed the sea, healed the lame and people where made whole again with his words.

> "The tongue has the power of life and death, and those who love it will eat its fruit."
> —Proverbs 18:21, NIV

It came to me that in the past, whenever I was facing a giant—I was going it alone. God and love were left out of my life. The martyrdom practiced on behalf of myself served no one, especially the idea of love. I had become a "legend in my own mind," and pride was eating away at me. My *faith on fire* was vanishing, and I needed to fuel my faith muscle. I needed a rekindle of my *faith on fire*. I had forgotten some of the most important lessons from firefighters and from my charming Sam.

When researching how to stay positive in the face of problems, I turned up many affirmations and Scriptures. I made myself a CD filled with these positive quotes. Every positive word that I could think of; every positive Scripture and idea I had ever thought of, or could find, I included it in the CD. I blended them together poetically with soft relaxing music. It is quite an amazing little product and effective even in its raw form. It was programming for hardheads of which I was an expert.

My goal was to impregnate my mind with thoughts of positive faith and expectancy, like I had learned early on in this department when fighting fire. Listening to the CD started working. I was excited! Life was good. Everything was great. I was positive and nothing could stop me. Then something stopped me—*me*.

The real test came when I got super busy with my company, and I quit focusing on staying positive. Again, I forgot whom I served—a God of love. I chose to serve anger and fight instead.

> "A new command I give you: Love one another. As I have loved you,
> so you must love one another."
>
> —John 13:34, NIV

Every single problem I had faced had been nothing more than an impossible situation waiting to turn into a miracle. When my faith was on fire, I faced the impossible and witnessed miracle after miracle. I realized the words spoken to me by my friend and Pastor George Hancock had become my mantra.

*"The first ingredient of a miracle is an impossible situation."*

Understanding a miracle is not defined by an event. A miracle is defined by the gratitude experienced when witnessing such an event. If we do not look for miracles, they do not appear. My miracle came from the inside out.

I realized that I already had the life I always wanted, but I had smudged it with my unruly thoughts and tongue when facing some overwhelming, impossible situations. I just needed to wake up and live the dream positively and powerfully like I was trained at Station 3.

Firefighters taught me to expect miracles by the way they approached their life of fighting fire. They did not sit back and whine about this big ole fire and all the work it was going to take. They got excited to dance with the devil, they met him head on, and they knew without a shadow of a doubt the fire would go out. It was *faith on fire!* I needed this firefighter way of being to show up again in my own life.

Our problems really are miracles waiting to happen. It is our destiny to believe in the last minute miracle, to look for it, to gut it up and put our *faith on fire* into action.

Life became rich with possibility and finally, after all these years of impossible situations, I got my miracle and retired.

*A girl's retirement with a man's pension—Miracle!*

When retiring, I realized I had left a trail for hundreds of women who were in emergency operations inside the Dallas Fire Rescue Department. The caliber of women in our department is awesome. All these women are playing powerful games in their lives and along with the necessary *faith on fire* attitudes. A lot of these women have made rank, and I would gladly follow them. I am leaving my citizens in good hands.

*Double miracle!*

My retirement party had everyone important in my life and career present—family, life-long friends and co-workers who are precious to me. We cut the cake with a big ole firefighter's ax. I am warmed by the sweet spirits of support. Some of the firefighters that showed up go way back to the days at Station 3.

How much better can life be? I lived fast and furiously inside this department with my *faith on fire* and many of life's important lessons are now under by belt. So not only my God, my parents, Coach Meadows and my Sam get credit for who I have become. The members of the Dallas Fire Rescue Department get credit too.

My heart is full, and God is good. I realized that my life has been like drinking out of a fire hose the entire time, and I still cannot drink it all in.

*Triple miracle!*

## Chinese Cracked Pot

The term *crackpot*, a mad, foolish or eccentric person, is not to be confused with a *cracked pot* which contained lead. We all might have a little cracked pot in us. Let me explain cracked pot with this Chinese fable.

A water bearer in China had two large pots, each hung on the ends of a pole which he carried across his neck. One pot had a crack in it, while the other pot was perfect and always delivered a full portion of water. At the end of a long walk from the stream to the house, the cracked pot arrived only half full.

For two years this went on daily, with the bearer delivering one and a half pots of water to his house. Of course the perfect pot was proud of its accomplishments, perfect for which it was made. The poor cracked pot was ashamed of its own imperfection, and miserable that it was able to accomplish only half of what it had been made to do.

After two years of bitter failure, the cracked pot spoke to the water bearer one day by the stream. "I am ashamed of myself, because this crack in my side causes water to leak out all the way back to the house."

The bearer said to the cracked pot, "Did you notice there were flowers only on your side of the path, but not on the other pot's side? That's because I have always known about your flaws, and I planted flower seeds on your side of the path. Every day while we walked back, you have watered these flowers for me. For two years I have been able to pick these beautiful flowers to decorate the table. Without you being just the way you are, there would not be this beauty to grace the house."

—Unknown

Moral: Each of us has our own unique flaws. We are all cracked pots. But it's the cracks and flaws we each have that make our lives together so very interesting and rewarding. You just have to take each person for what they are, and look for the good in them.

*There are a lot of cracked pots and champions in the Dallas Fire Rescue Department. We deliver like cracked pots and play and practice like champions!*

Thank you God for the moral to a story that would make my fast-paced life of living on the edge, wading through the bowels of hell, and taking my imperfections and cracks only to see them turn to miracles. I have lived to see impossible situations of which I am one, turn for the good into marvelous, amazing miracles.

## Refiner's Fire

"I have refined you, but not in the way silver is refined. Rather, I have refined you in the furnace of suffering. I will rescue you for my sake—yes, for my own sake!"

—Isaiah 48:10–11, NLT

While every fire is destructive, not all fire is bad. Refining really is reduction through high-temperature from a blasting furnace that is extremely hot and painful, but it can be critical to our personal growth and faith.

*Thank you God for turning up the heat in my life.*

Refining consists of purifying an impure material. The final, refined material is chemically identical to the original material, only it is purer—without dross, waste or impurities. Also involved is a stirring process that allows the impurities (dross) to come to the surface where it can be lifted and removed. I suppose refining could also be referred to as a separation process. It is where we are separated from the things that keep us from being pure, positive and powerful.

God knows what it takes to devour our nature. God knows how much heat it takes to melt our hearts.

*My heart is now melted and cooled.*

Separating the dross was a painful experience for me. I could face fire, but I did not want to face or reveal the real me. I was frightened of what I could be or become. I was frightened of all the possibilities.

When I was focused on the problems of life, I was so glued to keeping my eyes on those situations, that I would lose focus on the important thing—love. I would dwell on the impossible situations, and it caused me to ignore the miracles in my life. If a miracle did happen, I would not have been able to see it.

*There is nothing like the moment when you realize you have been absolutely wrong.*

Clearly, I had been wrong to take offense at the deputy's words. Mainly because, if my intentions are to walk in newness of light as a child of God, I needed to act like I had God in my own life and forgive him as I have been forgiven. I needed to recognize failure as failure, put it into perspective and forgive myself too. After all, meeting failure along the way of life is what keeps us grounded and moves us toward a successful, winning end. So, I lost my way, but clung to faith as it was all I had at the time.

"Fire tests the purity of silver and gold, but the Lord tests the heart."
—Proverbs 17:3, NLT

## Faith on Fire

*Faith on fire* is a winner's attitude that looks forward with hope, back with forgiveness, up with gratitude, down with compassion and in every direction gives love away. I was taught this lesson by firefighters and my life will be forever changed. I am forever thankful that my darkness turned to light, and my dream of retiring, writing this book, running Emergency Management Resources, LLC and speaking have all turned into reality.

"*Gut it up, Girl*," the words of the firefighters who sabotaged my mask, were transformed from the impossible into a mantra and a miracle. I gutted it up alright, and this adversity opened the door of opportunity for me many times over. I learned to get things done when others would not. I moved when others would not move. I grew stronger and stronger because of those words. It is amazing that something designed to be hurtful became one of my miracles. I used those impossible and negative words designed to hurt me, over and over throughout my life and career as a positive. I am simply assigning a different meaning to them, which is a miracle in my own thinking.

Sherrie's Retirement Shadow Box

The Dallas Fire Rescue Department has supported minorities, including myself. When looking back on all the racial divide, this impossible situation has become a miracle in that our department has a wide range of colors, genders and ethnicities in leadership. Our department reflects the citizens we serve, and I am proud to be a part of such a colorful blending of teammates. I realize when going through some of these perceived impossible situations, I should have been looking for the miracles.

In one year alone I documented over one hundred miracles in my life—but that is a story for another book.

For more than thirty-five years, I have seen members of the Dallas Fire Rescue Department push themselves from ordinary to extraordinary and together create miracles every single day. God was literally working in our lives, and our faith was strong and powerful when we focused on the more important things—love and respect of one another. My success and longevity in the fire rescue business was nothing but by the grace of God, and to Him I am thankful and my heart is filled with gratitude.

*Faith on Fire*

Today, I woke to face an impossible fire

Head held high, creating miracles my desire

My work was challenging and I would tire

At times things became an enormous quagmire

But, a change of heart, revelation was required

Years of living fast and furious I would retire

Learning to celebrate love in the face of fire

Is living full out, with my *faith on fire*

To members of the Dallas Fire Rescue Department, current or retired, you will forever remain lovingly in my prayers. I thank you and honor you for your warm-hearted kindness, acceptance and the overwhelming joy we shared over the years. You taught me some of the greatest lessons in life, especially, your example of an amazing winning attitude—*faith on fire.*

Sherrie's retirement gift – mounted firefighters axe

There is no doubt my divine design was to be a rescuer. It was woven into the fabric of my being. Now that I am retired, my divine design has morphed into a new challenge. It is clear that I must take these awesome lessons learned from the brotHERhood of firefighters back into my civilian life.

My future requires me to share the winning attitude of *faith on fire*. To teach others to accept the darkness and negativity in life and be determined to stay positive and live through it. To communicate pushing past the pain, playing and practicing like champions, while looking for the miracles inside the impossible.

To the citizens of the world, when disaster calls and you can no longer handle your impossible situation, go ahead—make the call to 911. Then pray that your firefighter or paramedic have their *faith on fire*. After all, our intention is to come to your impossible situation—creating miracles.

When finding the light, you must pass through the deepest of darkness. You have a destiny, but do you have the faith to follow it? I believe you do, and I speak miracles into your impossible situations!

# LESSONS FROM A FIREFIGHTER

1. The winner's attitude is expressed as *faith on fire*. Winners look forward with hope, back with forgiveness, up with gratitude, down with compassion and in every direction give love away.

2. There are those that think they can and there are those that think they can't. They are both right. Firefighters living inside faith on fire think "we can!"

3. We are *faith on fire* champions and we play and practice like champions! Firefighters play a bigger game and we make positive contributions to our citizens and each other.

4. Our *faith on fire* is called upon when we face darkness and negativity. We are determined to stay positive and live through darkness, because out of darkness is light. Out of light is love. Out of love is forgiveness. Out of forgiveness is unity.

5. We push through the pain with our *faith on fire* because it is what separates the winners from the losers.

6. A moment of impossible agony is worth a lifetime of the lessons from which we learn. The first ingredient of a miracle really is an impossible situation!

7.  We look for miracles in life. We see the tiny miracles and believe. We see the bigger miracles and grow. We speak miracles and witness lives being completely transformed.

8.  Firefighters have *faith on fire*, we pray and we believe in God because he can do more in a split second than we could ever do in our lifetime.

# CONTACT INFORMATION

## REDEMPTION
### PRESS

To order additional copies of this book,
or to schedule Sherrie to come speak at your event, please visit:
www.faithonfire.com or www.sherriecwilson.com
*Faith On Fire* screenplay is known as "Trial By Fire."

www.redemption-press.com.
Also available on Amazon.com and BarnesandNoble.com
Or by calling toll free 1-844-2REDEEM.